Harrowing Haunts

EMBEDDED WITH THE PARANORMAL PARAMILITARY

Riding with Mediums, Spirit Seekers, and Ghost Hunters

John Kachuba

ROSEN
PUBLISHING

New York

This edition published in 2017 by:

The Rosen Publishing Group, Inc.
29 East 21st Street
New York, NY 10010

Library of Congress Cataloging-in-Publication Data

Names: Kachuba, John B., author.
Title: Embedded with the paranormal paramilitary : riding with mediums, spirit seekers, and ghost hunters / John Kachuba.
Description: New York : Rosen Publishing, 2017. | Series: Harrowing haunts | Includes bibliographical references and index.
Identifiers: LCCN 2016010395 | ISBN 9781499463934 (library bound)
Subjects: LCSH: Ghosts.
Classification: LCC BF1461 .K325 2016 | DDC 133.1--dc23
LC record available at http://lccn.loc.gov/2016010395

Manufactured in China

Embedded with the Paranormal Paramilitary: First published as *Ghosthunters* by New Page Books/Career Press, copyright © 2007 John Kachuba.

For Emory Charles

AUTHOR'S NOTE

Most of the people I interviewed for this book were willing to have their names in print. A few, however, requested that I not use their real names when telling their stories. In such cases, I invented a name. These invented names are followed by an asterisk (*).

CONTENTS

INTRODUCTION

It's never good news when the phone rings at 2 a.m. This call was no exception.

"John! Dude, I don't believe it!"

The dude—me—didn't recognize the man's voice.

"Me and my friend? We're at this old farmhouse?"

Aha. I could see where this conversation was heading.

"And it's haunted...."

Bingo.

"And something—oh my God—something or someone's throwing crap off the roof at us!"

"Do you know what time it is?" I asked.

"Oh, sorry, dude. It's just so awesome! I found your name and number on the Internet and thought I'd call you. Did I wake you?"

Of course not, I thought. I'm The Ghosthunter. I wait by my phone 24/7 for your call.

"How about you e-mail me tomorrow all about your adventure?" I said.

"That's cool. I'll do it. Talk to you soon, dude."

"Be safe," I said, and I meant it, because I was sure these boys had partaken of some spirits of their own. With luck, they wouldn't remember this phone call the next morning. I've gotten used to these kinds of phone calls. And to equally strange e-mails. And photos. And to being haunted by "fans." Such is the life of a ghosthunter.

It wasn't always this way. Up until only a few years ago I had been a writer, quietly doing writerly things in a writerly way, not making much of a fuss, flying below the radar. I can't say that I spent much time thinking about ghosts. But when my editor buddy Jack Heffron asked me to write a series of ghost books, the ectoplasm really hit the fan.

I spent a good chunk of 2003 crisscrossing Ohio as I researched my first ghost book, Ghosthunting Ohio. In 2004, my travels took me through Illinois for Ghosthunting Illinois. In 2005 and 2006, as I was

John Kachuba and his wife, Mary Newman, with the Ghosthuntermobile at The Ridges in Athens, Ohio.
Courtesy of John Kachuba.

working on this book, I expanded my activities to include locations all across the country.

Through these years I have visited at least 100 haunted locations, often accompanied by my wife, Mary, a no-nonsense professor of environmental health. I came face to face with many people who had seen ghosts and told me their stories. Some of these people I initially discovered by visiting the myriad ghost sites on the Internet; others I found by word of mouth. I was amazed at how open people were to my questions; several of my subjects told me they had never revealed their stories to anyone else before, and that they were surprised to be doing so with me. Perhaps my low-tech approach, using pen and notebook, occasionally a tape recorder, made them feel less intimidated. Maybe I'm just a friendly guy. Many people also shared with me their photos and videotapes of ghostly phenomena.

Along the way I met psychics, mediums, "professional" ghosthunters, "certified" ghosthunters, spiritualists, ghost tour operators, and other assorted denizens of the paranormal world. Though I was a novice in that world, the very fact that I was writing books about it somehow gave me instant credibility. It made me an authority, and fair game for anyone with a story to tell.

I appreciated all those stories. The people who shared them with me were sincere, convinced in every case that they had had a brush with the paranormal. They came from all walks of life: schoolteachers, policemen, librarians, hotel clerks, waitresses, security guards, judges, and retired nuns. Yes, they believed, and I believed they believed. How could I doubt the word of a nun? Naturally, some of their stories wound up in my books. But others....

There was the woman who called me from her double-wide along the Ohio River near Ironton, Ohio. She told me a phantom train ran through her yard at night, engine roaring, light flashing; that a baby's voice cried from the long abandoned well on her property; that she found her son fast asleep and levitating 3 feet above his bed; and that her daughter was often visited by a "tall man with wings and red eyes." She told me that she herself had been visited by a spirit that broke into a million pieces when she invoked the name of Jesus for protection. Unfortunately, the pieces came together again, this time in the form of a towering devil that screamed profanities at her before disappearing. So, she wanted to know, could I come to her trailer and cleanse it of those ghosts?

No, I could not. I would not.

I did feel badly for her, though, and suggested she call a doctor (actually, I believe I said "psychiatrist") or her minister to help her. She told me they were all too afraid to come anywhere near her property. She was extremely depressed by the awful events unfolding in her trailer—as anyone would be—and that was why she was taking antidepressant medication. And tranquilizers. And smoking dope. Daily. I began to understand why she was seeing ghosts.

But for every one of those characters there were many more dedicated believers, people who wanted to talk with me because they wanted to hear about and share my adventures in ghostland, perhaps compare paranormal notes with me as they tried to understand what they had experienced. Until I started writing about it, in effect taking my own interest in the subject public, I never truly comprehended just how popular ghosts were in our culture.

One day not too long ago Mary and I drove our 1987 Buick Skyhawk, painted all over with ghosts and tombstones, to the former mental asylum in Athens, Ohio, where we now live (in Athens, not the asylum). The hospital's grounds encompass hundreds of acres, much of which is now covered with hiking trails. We parked the Ghosthuntermobile at a trailhead. No one else was around, but I had tucked a few Ghosthunting Ohio promotional postcards under a wiper blade in case any interested parties happened along. When we got back from our hike, half a dozen college kids were gathered around the car.

"Hey, are you John Kachuba?" one of them called out before we reached the car.

I'm always leery about answering that question when challenged by strangers, but I bravely answered that I was indeed John Kachuba, in the flesh. The kids were excited. They said they had been waiting for me for more than an hour and a half. They had seen the car and taken a postcard from the windshield. One of the girls in the group called a friend on her cell phone and asked the friend to check out my website, whose address was printed on the card. The friend did so, reading the information from my site over the phone to the girl. Now that I'd materialized, the kids plopped right down in the street by the Ghosthuntermobile and peppered me with questions about ghosts and hauntings.

"What was the scariest ghost you ever met?"

"How can you tell if your house is haunted?"

"Can anyone see ghosts?"

"Since clothes can't last forever, how come ghosts aren't naked?"

I was not able to answer a single question fully; they came so fast and furiously. After they had exhausted their questions, we shook hands all around (one student bought a book from the stash I keep in the Ghosthuntermobile) and they left.

"Just another Ghosthunter fan club meeting," Mary said, by now accustomed to the modest degree of notoriety that sometimes intrudes itself into our daily life. Previous to writing the books, I had no idea how popular ghost stories were, nor did I expect to be sought out by people looking for advice or just wanting to share their stories. Now both Mary and I have come to expect it as part of the life of a ghosthunter.

I'm always surprised when as many as 50 people will crowd into a little room in some small-town library to hear me talk about ghosts—though it's not entirely me they've come to hear. They come to hear each other, really, to reinforce each other in their belief. I have yet to give a talk in which people in the audience didn't come with ghost stories of their own, often documented with well-worn photos. Sometimes, I've felt that I was merely the moderator of a paranormal town meeting.

After one such talk at the public library in Nelsonville, Ohio, several people broke out photos they had taken of ghosts in their homes. They asked me to look at them and then passed them around to each other. For some reason, most of the photos of unexplainable mists and blurs were taken in their kitchens, which made me wonder about two things: Did ghosts need to eat? And why did so many people still have avocado-colored appliances?

I don't fully understand this fascination with ghosts, but I think I may be learning more about it. Perhaps the current popularity of ghosts and ghost stories—as evidenced by the best-selling books of psychic Sylvia Browne, along with TV shows such as John Edward's *Crossing Over,*

Medium, Ghost Hunters, Weird Travels, Most Haunted, and *Ghost Whisperer,* and movies such as *The Amityville Horror* and *Haunted Mansion*—has something to do with the times in which we live. Could it be that some of us, confronted with the daily nastiness of life (tsunamis, hurricanes, the war in Iraq, starvation, AIDS in Africa—you name it) brought to us through TV news or the newspapers, take hope in the idea of ghosts, seeing them as a sign that there's another chance for us after this life? If ghosts exist, wouldn't that prove we have immortal souls or spirits, and that there just might be a better place waiting for us once we're done here? That's a powerful message, especially for anyone troubled by the host of ills that surround us. Or maybe it's less philosophical than that—a harmless diversion, something to take our minds away from the realities of the world, if only for a few, scary moments. Whatever the reasons, most of us believe in ghosts, at least according to a 2003 Harris Poll of 2,201 adults, which showed that 51 percent of responders believe ghosts exist.

Such statistics ring true with my experiences as The Ghosthunter. This gig has been, and continues to be, a mind-expanding experience. I have learned that there are some crazies out there in the ghost world, but no more than there are bare-chested Cincinnati Bengals fans, or Jerry Springer show guests, or *Rocky Horror Picture Show* wannabes, or even NASCAR lovers. But there are also many more serious-minded, rational people who have been convinced by their own encounters that ghosts walk among us.

As for me, I remain something of a skeptic, but perhaps not as hard and fast about my skepticism as I had been before. After all, it's difficult to remain skeptical when everyone around you is caving in. It wasn't until after *Ghosthunting Ohio* was published that my two daughters told me that they had each experienced a ghost encounter years before, when they were in college. My sister-in-law told me she grew up in a haunted house. On the day I finished writing this Introduction, I got a haircut and Liz, the stylist, told me that a ghost once tapped her on the shoulder. She had also seen a little boy phantom with a lantern on a lonely country road at 3 a.m.

Moreover, I can honestly say that in my last three years of ghosthunting, I have had some weird experiences that I cannot fully explain. I have been on paranormal investigations in which strange lights have been recorded on videotape and disembodied voices have been heard on audiotape.

I've picked up spirit orbs in some of my photos and have heard ghostly whisperings and a phantom wind. All chinks in my armor of skepticism.

So, all I can say is that some unusual things are going on and that they may be far more common than I would have expected. See for yourself. The next time you're in the company of five or more family or friends, ask the group if anyone has ever had an encounter with ghosts. I'd be willing to bet my official *Ghosthunter* hat that someone will have a story. You may even discover some skeletons—I mean ghosts—in the family closet. Let me know if you hear a good story. I'm easy to find. Just check your local cemetery some dark and stormy night, and there I'll be.

John Kachuba
Athens, Ohio

CHAPTER 1
GHOSTOLOGY 101

Facts and trivia about ghost lore abound. What do you know about ghosts? Take this short quiz to test your knowledge. The answers to these questions appear at the end of this chapter.

1. What is the name of Casper the Friendly Ghost's girlfriend?
   a. Boolinda
   b. Wendy the Good Little Witch
   c. Morticia
   d. Lucy

2. How did Marian and George, the ghosts from the 1950s TV sitcom *Topper*, die?
   a. avalanche
   b. car accident
   c. suicide
   d. drowning

3. What type of vehicle did the Ghostbusters drive?
   a. Hummer
   b. station wagon
   c. ambulance
   d. hearse

4. How many ghosts visited Ebenezer Scrooge in Charles Dickens's *A Christmas Carol*?

    a. 2

    b. 1

    c. 4

    d. 3

5. Who played the pseudo-psychic Oda Mae in the 1990 film *Ghost*?

    a. Cher

    b. Margot Kidder

    c. Demi Moore

    d. Whoopi Goldberg

6. According to legend, which one of these can't a ghost cross?

    a. running water

    b. a highway

    c. a cemetery fence

    d. a mountain

7. A "noisy ghost" is also called a _____.

    a. wraith

    b. phantom

    c. medium

    d. poltergeist

8. Which phrase appears in the Gordon Lightfoot song "If You Could Read My Mind"?

    a. "about a ghost with a story to tell"

    b. "about a ghost from a wishing well"

    c. "about a ghost condemned to hell"

    d. "about a ghost whose feet don't smell"

9. The spooky attraction at Disneyland is called _____.

    a. Mystery Manor

    b. Hill House

    c. Haunted Mansion

    d. Fright Mansion

10. What do the letters T-A-P-S from TV's *Ghost Hunters* stand for?
    a. Trans Atlantic Psychic Society
    b. The Abnormal Psychical Society
    c. The Associated Parapsychic Society
    d. The Atlantic Paranormal Society
11. Who wrote *The Exorcist*?
    a. Stephen King
    b. William Peter Blatty
    c. Peter Straub
    d. Dean Koontz
12. A person who can hear ghosts is said to be a _____.
    a. ghost whisperer
    b. crazy person
    c. magus
    d. clairaudient

That wasn't too bad, was it? You may have noticed that many of the questions were about ghosts as we know them through "pop culture"— that is, through popular television programs and movies, books, music, and even amusement parks. Only three of the questions (6, 7, and 12) transcend pop culture and are part of the body of knowledge that makes up ghostology, the study of ghosts.

Most of us probably know what we know about ghosts through pop culture, rather than as a result of a dedicated study of parapsychology. Movies such as *Ghostbusters*, *The Ring*, *The Amityville Horror*, and *The Haunted Mansion*, along with such television programs as *Ghost Hunters*, *Medium*, *Ghost Whisperer*, and *Most Haunted* have made ghosts and hauntings more popular than ever. Add to this ghostly stories penned by novelists Stephen King, Peter Straub, and William Peter Blatty, along with nonfiction books by Sylvia Browne and the late Edgar Cayce, and we find ourselves buried beneath a mountain of ectoplasmic media.

We've all been exposed to it, even from our youngest days. I remember looking in my closet and under my bed every night for monsters and ghosts before going to sleep, my parents standing guard in my room until I gave them the "all clear." I remember an overnight at summer camp, sitting around a campfire listening to the teenaged counselors telling us about the "green googie ghost," whatever that was. I still don't know what it was, but back then it made for a very long night. I watched ghost movies, read ghost books, and scared the stuffing out of myself. To my great relief, I discovered that not all ghosts were mean and scary. There was the nice ghostly couple, Marian and George, on the television show Topper. There was Casper the Friendly Ghost, from comic books, although I did think that bubble-headed phantom was a whiner and a bit too wimpy for even my scaredy-cat sensibilities. As I grew older, I became aware of the classic ghost stories of Washington Irving, Charles Dickens, Nathaniel Hawthorne, Edith Wharton, and Henry James, whose Turn of the Screw remains, for my money, the best ghost story ever written.

Although most of us have shared similar experiences, there are many people who have gone beyond pop culture and have developed a body of knowledge about ghosts based on serious inquiry and research. Parapsychologists, paranormal investigators, mediums, psychics, and spiritualists have all contributed their discoveries and findings to the field of ghostology. It is to these experts that we must turn to understand the nature of ghosts.

What Is a Ghost?

There are different theories about the nature of ghosts, but one simple way to define them is to say that a ghost is the spirit of a person who was once alive. Even this bland statement can be challenged to some degree, because the meaning of "spirit" may differ from one person to another. For our purposes, we will define "spirit" as the eternal essence of a person that survives death and goes on forever in some form.

Almost every religious creed maintains some belief in an afterlife, a realm after death in which the dead person's spirit lives on. For Christianity and some other faiths, the type of afterlife reserved for the spirit depends upon the type of life the person lived on Earth. Thus, in Christianity at least, a good person's spirit is rewarded in Heaven; a bad person's spirit is punished in Hell. The essential point here, however, is not about reward or punishment, but is about the basic assumption that the spirit lives on after death. No Christian would question that.

Christian theology is full of references to spirits, and here another distinction should be drawn between spirits and ghosts. Spirits, such as angels and demons, are discarnate beings that never had a human existence. Ghosts, on the other hand, are discarnate beings who were at one time human. Catholic theology, at least, rejects ghosts and communication with the dead, yet stories of miraculous appearances to the living made by the Virgin Mary as well as many other saints abound. The New Testament itself describes how Jesus suddenly appeared to the apostles on the road to Emmaus after his death, and in the sealed and shuttered upstairs room as well. At the risk of being burned at the stake as a heretic, may I say that all these appearances seem, well, ghostly? They are certainly similar in content and detail to contemporary ghost stories.

Members of other faiths also assume the spirit lives on after death.

Hindus believe that the spirit is reborn again after death in another body—the process known as reincarnation. In Hindu belief, the soul or spirit of the deceased person hovers near the body for a time in a liminal state of ghosthood. Funerary rites over the next several days involve food and water offerings in order to rebuild a "body" in which the spirit may traverse the world of the living on its way to return to the ancestors, where it will eventually become reborn.

Buddhists, too, believe the spirit is repeatedly reincarnated until it finally attains enlightenment, nirvana, and is freed from the cyclical process. There is also a time of ghosthood in Buddhist philosophy. According to their beliefs, there are eight stages of death. In the final stage, the spirit separates from the body, but does not immediately become reincarnated. The spirit is not even aware that its mortal self has died and may try to speak to or interact with living friends and family. The spirit is confused and can travel anywhere instantaneously without obstruction. Further, it maintains its five senses, even though it has no physical body. This state of ghosthood is said to last no more than 49 days. During those days the living relatives of the dead person offer prayers that the spirit may find a good person into which it will be reborn.

The Spiritualist Church has at the core of its philosophy the belief that each one of us lives after death and that our spirits may be contacted by the living to offer advice, guidance, comfort, and support. Ghosts are an accepted fact among Spiritualists and are not to be feared. An elderly Spiritualist minister I met during my research told me that she had grown up with ghosts, saw them all the time, and was thoroughly accustomed to communicating with them. She had no fear of them, telling me that she feared the living far more than any ghost. At Spiritualist services, mediums routinely impart messages from those who have "passed," as the Spiritualists say, to members of the congregation.

The religious beliefs and traditional tales of billions of people in various cultures worldwide seem to allow for the possibility that ghosts do exist. It is also entirely possible, of course, that the accumulated wisdom of countless generations from all around the world regarding a belief in some kind of life after death is just plain wrong. A skeptic could say that such a belief is invented simply to help us cope with the chilling idea that life comes to an abrupt end at the grave, that without such a belief life would be worthless and without meaning.

These people are not invited to parties.

Even if we assume these religious traditions are correct in asserting a spiritual life after death, they shed little light on the nature of ghosts.

For that, we can turn to science.

I have no idea whether or not Albert Einstein believed in ghosts, but some of his theories in the realm of physics may support their existence. Einstein proved that all the energy of the universe is constant and that it can neither be created nor destroyed. Energy can, however, be transformed from one type of energy into another, a process that takes place all the time. Further, Einstein proved that everything is made up of energy. Even a seemingly solid sheet of steel is composed of an invisible galaxy of madly swirling atoms generating energy. The human body is no less a mass of energy produced by the billions upon billions of atoms that make up its corporeal reality. So what happens to that energy when we die? If it cannot be destroyed, it must then, according to Dr. Einstein, be transformed into another form of energy. What is that new energy? How does it look? The being that used to be me is broken down into its raw components, energy "leaking" out in the various states of decomposition as pure elements. But is that all that happens? What of the energy that composed our spirit, our spiritual essence? What happens to that?

Consider the possibility that the energy of that spiritual essence continues on in some way, or is transformed to a state of energy that does not require a corporeal state. Could we call that new creation a ghost? Most psychic researchers are convinced that ghosts are beings of pure energy. They document a ghostly presence by fluctuations in electromagnetic frequency as recorded on electromagnetic frequency (EMF) meters. Some researchers believe that ghosts, creatures of energy that they are, feed off other energy sources to "live," thus explaining the blown fuses, exploded light bulbs, and dead batteries that occur on so many paranormal investigations.

A second theory of physics, courtesy once again of Dr. Einstein, may offer us another clue as to whether or not ghosts exist. Einstein proved that light moves at a speed of 186,000 miles per second, or 700 million miles an hour. To give you an idea how fast that is, the distance from the Earth to the moon is about 239,000 miles; the light from a switched-on flashlight would reach the moon in less than one and a half seconds. Nothing can move faster than the speed of light. Another strange effect of the speed of light, one that I won't even pretend to understand, is that time slows down as an object or person accelerates toward the speed of light. We've all seen the sci-fi movies or Twilight Zone dramas in which a space traveler blasts off from Earth and returns many years later to find his wife has grown old and died, and his children are senior citizens, whereas he has hardly aged a day since he departed. Can this amazing phenomenon somehow support the existence of ghosts?

All right. Strap yourself in while I try to explain. It's going to be a bumpy ride.

Could it be possible that some of that spiritual essence I talked about, once it is freed from the body as energy, approaches speeds that come close to the speed of light? If that were so, then the energy would be slowed down, in a sense held back in time and space. Further, if that energy still retains its spiritual nature, then would that not mean that there would exist some spiritual being still bound in our realm, a being we might call a ghost? Wouldn't this theory of a slowed-down entity unable to escape Earthly bonds also provide an explanation for why ghosts are often seen throughout many years before finally disappearing?

Or, do I just need to sit down and get a grip?

Though I do believe that, as Einstein proved, the energy that is "I" goes on in some unfathomable way after death, I don't have the words to articulate what that means. I am also embarrassed to admit that I do not have the imagination to conceive what existence would be like after death.

Why Do Ghosts Exist?

Everyone passes into a spiritual form after death, but not everyone becomes a ghost. Why is it that some people remain as earthbound ghosts, rather than passing on to a new existence in the afterlife? One popular theory for why there are ghosts says that ghosts are the spiritual remains of people who are unable to cross over into the afterlife ("crossing over into the light," as paranormal investigators would say) for various reasons. These ghosts are stuck on Earth because they have some unfinished business left to accomplish, and whatever that business is, it is so important to the ghosts that these poor shades are tied to the mortal world until such time as someone with the ability releases them to the light. The unfinished business is usually of a personal nature (a mother worried about leaving her children, a husband worried about leaving his wife, a person who has not had time to rectify a wrong he committed). The ghost is in no position to conclude its business, of course, but it is not aware of its limitations and must be convinced that its concerns are no longer valid before it can finally cross over.

Another theory states that ghosts are the spirits of people who either do not know they are dead, or simply refuse to accept that reality. These are frequently the ghosts of people who have died unexpectedly, or at an age much younger than would have been typically expected. These ghosts, too, must be convinced of their true status by someone with that ability and persuaded to cross over.

Ghosts may also exist because we will them to exist. This act of will is not usually a conscious act, but springs from deep within our own psyches. It may be possible that people who have suffered the loss of someone dear to them and who are having a great deal of trouble accepting that loss, could create ghosts in their own minds that appear to them as very real beings. Similarly, people with certain mental disorders, such as schizophrenia, are subjected to hallucinations and delusions that may carry all the hallmarks of ghosts and hauntings. But then, there is the odd case of the tulpa, a ghost that is consciously created through long periods of meditation, and once created, takes on a ghostly existence independent of its contemplative creator. None of these ghosts are merely "in our own heads," as we shall see in subsequent chapters.

How Do Ghosts Manifest Themselves?

Despite all the popular representations of sheet-draped, chain-rattling ghosts, seeing an apparition, as a fully visible ghost is called, is not at all common. Still, this manifestation, either whole or in part, of an actual ghost, is our most common idea of a ghost. Full-body apparitions differ among observers, some people seeing them as smoky, semi-transparent images, and others seeing them as solidly as living persons. The difference could be due to either the observer's degree of sensitivity to paranormal experiences, or it could be due to the ghost's ability to manifest itself. In addition to full-body apparitions, many people have reported seeing only parts of a body. One person I interviewed spoke of seeing a pair of legs walk up stairs. Another spoke of seeing a shoulder appear in a hallway, and still another saw a head hovering over her bed. As in full-body apparitions, it may be that partial apparitions are caused by the observer's incomplete sensitivity to such things, or the ghost's inability to completely materialize. The latter raises the question of whether or not ghosts appear forever. Could it be that a partial apparition is the best an old ghost can do, and that at some point he will simply vanish? Or could the reverse be true: A new ghost slowly develops the ability to materialize?

Relatively common visual phenomena are shadow people, also called corner ghosts, which appear only briefly in the viewer's peripheral vision. Many of the people I have interviewed spoke of seeing something "off to one side" or from the "corner" of their eyes. The amount of detail that can be seen varies with the viewer. Some people describe only a shadow or mist; others can describe clothing, hairstyles, and other distinguishing characteristics of an individual.

Another visual phenomenon is the residual haunting, or psychic impression. A residual haunting is an image that plays itself back repeatedly over time, similar to looped videotape. The theory is that the energy associated with some event—often, but not always, a tragic one—attaches itself to the place in which it occurred and remains there for a long time. Under the right circumstances, the event manifests itself. The primary feature that distinguishes a residual haunting from an actual encounter with a ghost is that there is no interaction between the persons in the haunting and those observing it. The imaged persons in the haunting are seemingly unaware of their human observers. This is because the imaged persons in the residual haunting are not really present in the same way that a ghost may be. They are more "impressions" of people who have passed on than they are entities. People who experience a residual haunting will describe the persons or events they have witnessed in similar terms; it is this similarity common to many viewers that alerts the paranormal investigator to the presence of a residual haunting, rather than a haunting by a ghost.

Living ghosts is a term that applies to two different types of ghostly appearances. The first is when a person is visited by, and interacts with, a person, often a family member or friend, at the moment that person dies. The observer does not usually know at the time that the person is deceased, but finds out later and often discovers that the precise time of death was exactly the time when the deceased visited them. This type of event is generally thought of as the deceased person's farewell to loved ones. The second type of living ghost experience is when a person is visited by a family member or friend who is alive, but in need of help. It could be that the person is ill, or suffering in some other way, and is seeking a psychic connection to a loved one to help get him/her through whatever problems he/she is experiencing. This seeking of assistance is not made consciously, and the person who appears as a living ghost has no recollection of that event. In some cases, the observers may see an image of themselves, either exactly as they appear or slightly changed in some way. A famous example of this phenomenon is Abraham Lincoln seeing two versions of his own face reflected in a mirror. In a conversation with his friend Noah Brooks (later retold by Brooks in Harper's New Monthly Magazine) Lincoln said:

> I saw myself reflected, nearly at full length; but my face, I noticed, had two separate and distinct images, the tip of the nose of one being about three inches from the tip of the other. I was a little bothered, perhaps startled, and got up and looked in the glass, but the illusion vanished. On lying down again I saw it a second time—plainer, if possible, than before; and then I noticed that one of the faces was a little paler, say five shades, than the other. I got up and the thing melted away, and I went off and, in the excitement of the hour, forgot all about it—nearly, but not quite, for the thing would once in a while come up, and give me a little pang, as though something uncomfortable had happened. When I went home I told my wife about it, and a few days after I tried the experiment again, when, sure enough, the thing came again; but I never succeeded in bringing the ghost back after that, though I once tried very industriously to show it to my wife, who was worried about it somewhat. She thought it was "a sign" that I was to be elected to a second term of office, and that the paleness of one of the faces was an omen that I should not see life through the last term.

Most people who have ghostly encounters experience the paranormal through senses other than the visual. It is typical for these people to hear unexplainable sounds—footsteps, whispering, knockings—or to detect scents they associate with the deceased—Uncle Herman's favorite pipe tobacco, or Grandma Sadie's lilac perfume, for example. Often ghosts are felt, rather than seen or heard. Cold spots in a house, the electric feeling of having your hair stand on end, the certain sensation that someone is behind you or watching you, and feeling the air around you as being thick or dense, may be manifestations of a phantom presence. Objects that move on their own, without any reasonable explanation such as wind or vibration, may also be indicators of a ghost at work.

Ghosts often manifest themselves through physical means. It is not uncommon for some object to suddenly appear during a séance or paranormal investigation. Small stones or coins have been reported to appear out of thin air and fall to the floor in haunted houses. Pieces of jewelry, photos, and other small personal objects that were either lost a long time ago, or are completely unfamiliar to the observer, may mysteriously turn up on a table or in a drawer. Such objects are called apports and are thought to indicate the presence of a ghost.

The champion at physical manifestation is the poltergeist, which is German for "noisy spirit." A poltergeist likes to knock on walls and bang doors, slam windows, knock pictures off walls, throw furniture around, start fires, and generally make a mess. Paranormal investigators remain divided on the nature of poltergeists. Some of them think poltergeists are troubled spirits looking for release; others doubt they are spirits at all, believing instead that troubled individuals, especially adolescents, subconsciously produce poltergeist effects through their own mental energy.

Who Are the Ghosthunters?

There are a variety of terms given to the people who populate the world of the paranormal. Although the title of this book loosely refers to them all as ghosthunters, I should more accurately define some of the terms used for these various people.

A ghosthunter or paranormal investigator is someone who studies ghostly phenomena in an attempt to understand the causes of the phenomena. A true ghosthunter does not automatically assume that ghosts exist, but first tries to rule out any logical or natural explanation for the phenomena. Only after that is done can he tackle the question of whether or not the phenomena were caused by a ghost. Ghosthunters may or may not have the natural ability to see, hear, or feel ghosts, and they will often use a variety of electronic equipment to aid them in their investigations. A ghostbuster is a person who investigates a haunted location with the intent of contacting the ghost and releasing it to the light, thereby removing it from the location.

A psychic is a person who has the ability to perceive things that cannot be perceived through normal use of the senses. A psychic who is clairvoyant receives detailed mental images of people and events he could not have known about through any other means, whereas a clairaudient psychic hears sounds and voices no one else can hear. An empathic psychic has the ability to feel the emotions of others, both living and dead.

A medium or channeler can bring forth a ghost by allowing the spirit to use its body and voice. The medium generally enters a trance or relaxed meditative state and gives up his physical self to the spirit. It is not uncommon for the medium's voice to change to that of the deceased person's, or for his facial expressions and posture to take on those of the spirit. In some cases, the medium may be able to create a materialization of the ghost separate from his body.

Parapsychologists are psychologists who study the evidence for such psychological phenomena as psychokinesis, telepathy, clairvoyance, and ghosts. Trained and educated in the scientific method, their studies are typically more complex and regimented than that of the paranormal investigator.

A spiritualist is a person who believes that the living may contact the spirits of the dead in order to seek their guidance, advice, or assistance. They may or may not be members of a Spiritualist church.

A demonologist studies ghostly phenomena to determine if it is caused by demons, rather than your garden-variety ghost. If the diabolical is involved, a demonologist will try to remove the entity from the premises. If the demon has taken possession of a person, the demonologist may resort to exorcism to rid the person of the demon.

Do You Believe in Ghosts?

What should matter for my readers, I think, is not so much what I believe as what the many people I have interviewed believe. There is no doubt in my mind that these people absolutely believe that what they saw, heard, or felt cannot be explained in any rational, logical way. They are convinced that their experiences can only be explained as a brush with the paranormal, with ghosts. Who am I to tell them otherwise? These people live in, work at, or regularly visit these haunted places and know them much more intimately than I. They have spent more time at these places than I ever did and are thus in a much better position to experience ghostly phenomena. Ghosts don't necessarily appear on demand, and it would be a rare occurrence for one to make itself known during a single investigation. Not impossible, but rare. Other ghosthunters have told me about repeatedly investigating a site purported to be haunted and spending hours there, photographing the place, taking tape recordings, and noting various types of measurements, only to find nothing that conclusively proved the existence of a ghost. In short, I took my interviewees at their words, and so should my readers.

Thousands of years ago, early man felt the earth tremble and quake, saw it split open before his very eyes, and believed those actions to be caused by angry gods, rather than sliding tectonic plates. The Ancient Chinese saw the sun disappear from the sky during an eclipse and believed that a dragon had swallowed it. I can listen to my favorite golden oldies station, and even though I can't see them, nor explain them, I believe that radio waves are out there bringing me those tunes. What I'm saying is that, smug as we may be due to our incredible 21st-century knowledge and technology, we are still learning; we are still developing technology. It may be that the weird and sometimes frightful actions we attribute to ghosts may simply be the palpable manifestations of some scientific principals we do not yet understand. Perhaps a new scientific discipline, ghostology, will emerge that will attach ghostly activities to rational and logical sources. The mystery of ghosts, and the thrill of chasing them, will be gone.

But what if science fails to explain them away, as it has failed to do thus far? That will keep you and me busy, won't it?

QUIZ ANSWERS

1. b
2. a
3. c
4. c
5. d
6. a
7. d
8. b
9. c
10. d
11. b
12. d

CHAPTER 2
ESTHER SPEAKS

Friday, May 13, 2005. It was dusk on an unseasonably warm day as Sherri Brake-Recco, her husband Frank Recco, and I bumped up the gravel road in Sherri's black Toyota 4 Runner. I was riding shotgun. Through the windshield I could see the daylight quickly fading behind the old blue farmhouse that squatted on a patch of lawn surrounded by fields left fallow. A handful of shaggy pine trees fringed the house.

Sherri Brake-Recco.
Courtesy of Sherri Brake-Recco.

"This is it," Sherri said, as she turned the Toyota onto the lawn. "I wonder if anyone is here yet."

"The lights are on inside," Frank said, leaning over the front seat.

We got out of the truck.

There was a pickup truck parked alongside a small outbuilding. Behind it stood a lone rusted silo, the top missing. I noticed dark clouds suddenly descending upon the forested hillsides in the distance, and felt a cold breeze spring up. A flash of lightning sliced through the gathering gloom. Thunder grumbled over the fields. A few drops of rain fell. Appropriate for Friday the 13th, I thought.

"Let's see if we can beat the rain," Sherri said. She opened the back of the truck to retrieve her equipment.

Frank and I didn't move.

As we stood there watching the storm swarm up over the hills, a towering figure came lumbering from around back of the outbuilding. A bear, I thought, but no—the figure was human. The guy stood 6 feet tall. He wore muddy work boots, jeans with suspenders, and an electric

Sherri Brake-Recco and Big Larry at the Old Blue Farmhouse.
Courtesy of John Kachuba.

blue T-shirt that could not prevent his belly from hanging over his belt. He came closer, revealing a gray Willie Nelson beard and blue and white bandana tied around a head of thinning hair.

He carried a rifle.

"We're dead," said Frank.

But the man didn't shoot. Instead, as the car carrying our other team members, Vince and Hannah, pulled in beside Sherri's truck, he offered to help us bring some of the gear inside the house. His name was Larry, and he maintained the abandoned farmhouse for the owner. We quickly dubbed him Big Larry, as the man who had asked Sherri to come out and investigate the farmhouse was also named Larry.

I figured it was a lucky thing he didn't shoot us in the rapidly gathering dark, and attributed our good luck to the bird that had defecated on my shirt only an hour before as we ate our dinner on the deck of a biker bar in town. Italian custom declares such a disgusting occasion—the bird crap, not the biker bar—to be auspicious. The cornfields of Ohio were a far cry from Italy, but I'm half Italian, so I went with it.

The rain was starting to come down harder now as we lugged the rest of our gear inside, piling it up on a table in the little parlor. Tripod, video-cam, digital cameras, tape recorders, EMF meters, thermometers, flashlights, dowsing rods, and, of course, chocolate chip cookies, coffee, and a cooler of cold drinks. We were prepared.

Sherri had been to the 1820s farmhouse once before with Frank, so she led the rest of us on a quick tour of the house. The room in which we gathered was small and square with a crazy-quilt pattern of at least four different kinds of wallpaper plastered over each other or peeling off the walls. Large bare patches broke up what remained of the wallpaper. In some places, the walls had rotted down to the lathing. On the wall above the table where we had dropped our gear were three shelves, upon which were arranged an odd assortment of objects d'junk: ceramic dogs and frogs—a lot of frogs—shotgun shells, a baseball, a flower pot, a little wooden car, a miniature lighthouse, and salt and pepper shakers.

To the right of this room was a parlor with the same designer wall treatment. A single, bare bulb on a shadeless lamp dimly lit the room. A beat-up blue recliner and saggy couch sat on the dusty wood floor. The window on the far wall was opened to the elements. In the weak light, a long tattered curtain flapped wildly in the wind, casting dancing shadows on the wall.

In the back half of the house was the kitchen, which contained a table, oven, and refrigerator. The ceiling here was cracked and flaking away, and sagged dangerously around the lamp suspended over the table. There was a door to the outside but it was sealed over with clear plastic sheeting, which was nailed to the wall. A good-luck horseshoe was hung above the door. An old summer kitchen opened off the back of the kitchen. It hadn't been used for many years and served now as a dark and dusty storage space.

Another empty room, perhaps a former bedroom, was located off the kitchen. Opening what I thought was a closet revealed a narrow flight of stairs to the second floor. Peering up, all I saw was darkness. Sherri and I crept up the stairs, our flashlights piercing the dark.

Frank remained downstairs with Vince and Hannah, walking around as if he were Frankenstein and making ghost noises. I think this was his way of coping with the house and whatever spirits it contained. A few weeks before, Frank, an avowed ghost skeptic, had accompanied his wife to the house, simply because he didn't want Sherri to go there alone. During their visit he saw a ghost, a grandmotherly type wearing an apron. She was standing in the doorway at the rear of the house looking at him. Then she was gone. Frank had had misgivings about going out to the house a second time, but decided maybe he could find an answer to whatever it was he had seen. Clowning around helped to calm his nervousness.

There were two bedrooms upstairs, both of them in bad condition. Sherri and I entered the first, at the front of the house.

"Oh man, do you feel that?" Sherri asked.

I did. As soon as we stepped into the room, I felt an oppressive heaviness in the air, almost as if I was underwater. But the feeling was not simply external. I felt uncomfortable pressure, a fullness deep within me, seated low in my belly, and I understood exactly what it meant when someone said he had "a gut feeling" about something.

"This room is really charged," Sherri said, setting a small lantern down on the floor.

A crash of thunder suddenly broke the oppressive stillness of the room. Lightning flashed outside, illuminating through the windows a line of trees being whipped by the wind. Rain pelted the roof above us. We played our lights around the room. An old carpet lay rolled up to one side of the room. In a corner, the wooden headboard of a small bed stood propped against the wall.

Then I heard the children. Muffled beneath the beating rain and rolling thunder, the sounds were indistinct at first, but as I moved closer to the headboard I could hear them more clearly.

"What is it?" Sherri said, watching me.

"Listen."

She came over to where I stood listening.

I heard high-pitched squealing and chattering, the sounds of children on a playground far away.

"What is that?" Sherri said.

I shook my head and shined my light into the corner and over the headboard. "I don't know," I said. "Critters of some kind, I guess. There must be all kinds of animals in these walls. Squirrels, raccoons, mice, who knows?"

"Probably, but this room's loaded with negative energy," she said. "I'm going to set up a camera in here."

She went downstairs for her equipment and returned with Frank. They set up the video recorder on the tripod in a corner of the room. We briefly checked out the rear bedroom, and then went back downstairs.

The other Larry—Little Larry—had just arrived, accompanied by a lady friend. He was the star of the show, because he had been the one to originally contact Sherri, telling her about the ghosts he had seen at the house and asking her to investigate. Little Larry was an older man, with gray hair and a thick gray moustache. He was a retired cop with 35 years on the force, and he was still dressed as one in black shoes and pants, and a black jacket. A soft-spoken man, his face bore a weary expression, as if he had been kept awake for a long time and had great worries troubling him.

Sherri had told me over the phone that Little Larry's ghost stories, as strange as they seemed, were consistent in their details, no matter how often he related them. That consistency made him more credible, she thought. As he sat on a folding chair in our "headquarters," nursing a cold coffee, he once again told us what he had seen, and sometimes, felt.

His first ghostly experience at the house occurred when he and his dog entered the very room where we were now gathered, and Little Larry sensed the presence of several "gangsters" there. He didn't actually see them as much as sense their presence.

"I was wearing my police uniform at the time," Little Larry said, "and I could feel that the spirits hated my guts." He was certain they meant to do him harm. He left the house in a hurry.

On another visit to the house, he saw a woman, surrounded by a Christmas wreath with lighted candles, peering down at him from an upstairs window. A different time, he saw a man wearing a Civil War uniform standing in an upstairs bedroom. Little Larry also saw two children in the house. These were apparently the same two children that Laura Wissler, a psychic friend of Sherri's, had seen in the front bedroom on Sherri's first visit there and had "released to the light," meaning that she had helped those poor ghosts find their way to peace.

Little Larry said he had researched the house and had documents "from Columbus," documents that we never saw, which verified several facts that might explain the hauntings: The house was used as a gang hangout during the Prohibition era; a previous owner who had lost a leg at Antietam during the Civil War fell out of the barn hayloft, broke his neck, and died; a man murdered his cheating wife in the front room; an Indian trading post existed on the site before the house was built and an entire family, including 13 children, were trapped inside the post and burned to death during an Indian raid, their bodies buried on the premises.

Little Larry had rented the house several years earlier, hoping to move in, but he never did. "I can't. They won't let me," he said, speaking of the ghosts. He and his buddy, Big Larry, now used the house as a sort of hunting cabin, but Little Larry said that he would never stay at the house by himself. This from a man who said he had seen ghosts all his life, including during his tour of duty in Vietnam.

There was still a member of our team missing. The psychic, Laura, and her husband had not yet arrived, no doubt delayed by the storm. We waited for her, listening to Little Larry's stories, now and then checking the house with the EMF meters, but getting no unusual results.

Sherri and I took a pair of dowsing rods to the bedrooms upstairs. The front bedroom still felt "heavy," although not as much as before. Using the dowsing rods I detected a spot in the room at which the rods crossed, indicating some source of energy. I walked through the spot and the rods uncrossed after a few steps. Every time I stepped back into the space, the rods crossed; when I came out, they uncrossed. I could find no apparent energy source that would have made the rods move, but I was aware of a pitch in the floor that I could not rule out as a factor in their movement. Sherri trained the EMF meter in the area without any odd results.

The rain had let up, so we decided to go outside to check the grounds and the barn. The whole group wandered out into the darkness. A line of tall pine trees marked the boundary between the back lawn and the fields. The trees were spaced evenly apart and had obviously been planted there by some former owner. It was there in a line between two of the trees that Sherri detected the bodies.

Little Larry had said that the victims of the Indian attack had been buried on the grounds. It was also possible that other owners of the farm and their families had been buried on the premises as well, family burial plots being common in earlier times. Now, while I held the flashlight on her, Sherri dowsed the area beneath the trees. As she walked a line between the trees, the rods crossed at three evenly spaced spots. She mapped out three areas of energy, each about 5 feet long, roughly the length of a body. She handed me the rods and I detected pretty much the same areas.

"I think there are bodies here," Sherri said, holding a single rod over one of the sites. "By their size, I would say they were young. Teenagers maybe, possibly younger than that." She turned to Little Larry. "Do you know if there were any burials in this spot?"

"Not for sure," he said. "The documents only say that people were buried on the property."

"What about the barn?" I asked. "Should we try there?"

Little Larry and his lady friend went back to sit on the porch of the house and wait for Laura. Big Larry led the rest of us through the field to the barn. Bats darted through the dark barn, caught briefly in our lights. I was still holding a pair of dowsing rods so I thought I'd give them a try in the barn. To my amazement, I found an area of energy about 8 feet by 5 feet.

"What the heck?" I said. I looked up and saw a smile on Big Larry's face. "What?" I asked him.

"You found the car," he said.

"The car?"

"He dowsed a car?" Sherri said. "What were you concentrating on?" she asked me.

"Nothing, just energy. Not a car, that's for sure. You mean there's a car buried down there?" I asked Big Larry. "Why?"

He shrugged, his shadow looming against the barn wall. "I don't know why. All I know is a previous owner had an old car that he dragged out here and buried."

"Was there anyone in it?" Sherri said, a reasonable question under the circumstances.

"Not that I've ever heard about," Big Larry said.

I was not completely reassured by his statement. Was there a body down there he hadn't heard about, sitting behind the wheel of some old junker? My ruminations were cut short when Sherri's cell phone rang. It was Laura. She and her husband were only a few miles away, so we exited the barn and made our way back to the house.

As we walked through the wet grass, I reviewed the evening as it had transpired thus far. What was going on at the old farmhouse? We had vague feelings of uneasiness in one room, the possibility of some bodies buried in the yard, a car buried in the barn, Frank and Little Larry's ghost stories, and, oh yes, Friday the 13th. I didn't know what to make of all that. Nothing added up.

Headlights approached the house. Laura and her husband had arrived. After greeting each of us, Laura went upstairs. Sherri and I followed her. In the front bedroom, approximately where I had dowsed an area of energy, Laura said that she felt something as well, although not as strong as it had been when she first came out to the house a few weeks before with Sherri. That was when she had sensed the two children in the room and sent them on their way to wherever it is that ghosts go to find peace.

So, what was the presence that still lingered there? I wondered.

I would soon find out.

Despite Sherri's reluctance to use Ouija boards, Laura had brought one with her. Many researchers do not like to use Ouija boards because, if used improperly or by the inexperienced, unwanted spirits may be accidentally contacted. In this instance we put our trust in Laura's psychic abilities to make sure we didn't get a paranormal wrong number when we dialed the great beyond.

We all crowded around the kitchen table. The room was dark, lit only by two small candles sitting on the table. Hannah and Little Larry's lady friend started us off, the board between them. Frank had set up the video recorder on its tripod and was recording the event.

To Laura's question ("Are there any spirits here?") the planchette lightly held by the two women slowly moved toward "yes" and stopped there. Laura asked for the name of the spirit guiding the planchette. It moved over to "E," paused there, then moved to "S," then "T," then wandered over the board, seemingly confused.

"Is your name Esther?" Laura asked.

Yes.

"Did you live in this house?"

Yes.

"Are you the person who Frank saw the last time he was here?"

Yes.

"When did you die?" said Laura.

1895.

Laura continued to ask Esther more questions, sometimes aided by questions from the rest of us. We took turns on the board, relieving each other when our arms got too tired. Esther's answers now were becoming confused, and we couldn't make sense of some of them. At one point Laura asked, "Do you want to be released to the light?"

The previously sluggish planchette whisked over to No.

"Excuse me," I said, "but shouldn't we be concerned about a spirit that doesn't want to be released?"

I thought I saw Sherri nod her head in agreement.

Just then Frank said that he was having trouble with the camera. It wouldn't stay in focus, even though he wasn't doing anything to change the focus. That didn't sound good either, I thought.

Laura looked thoughtful. "Okay, maybe one more question. Were those your children in the upstairs room?"

Laura may have touched upon a sore point with the ghost. The planchette came to a dead stop and would not move again. We had lost contact with Esther.

That concluded our evening of ghosthunting. As I rode back to the Recco house with Sherri and Frank, I thought about what had happened. Contacting Esther only added more strangeness to an evening that was already filled with seemingly random and unconnected strange events. I wondered if all ghosthunts were similar to this one, but finally came to the conclusion: How could they be any different? We were seeking logical explanations for what defied logic; logical connections for what could not be connected logically. Rationally. Further, we were getting only a glimpse of the bits and pieces of the house's 200-years-plus history. Of course they would make no sense to us.

Ghosthunting does not employ a scientific method, despite the technology used by many ghosthunters—our team included. It is more a method that relies upon the randomness of the universe, a good amount of dumb luck, and faith. The latter may be the most important.

CHAPTER 3
THE GREAT ASHEVILLE GHOST HUNT

Dusk was just beginning to settle in as I drove up the gravel drive of the Smith-McDowell house in Asheville, North Carolina. It was early June, the land still soggy from a heavy downpour courtesy of the remnants of Hurricane Cindy. The rhododendron bushes clumped along the wrought-iron fence separating the antebellum mansion from Victoria Road were in full bud, ready to flower at any moment. Tall oak

The haunted Smith-McDowell House in Asheville, North Carolina.
Courtesy of John Kachuba.

trees stood sentinel around the house, their ancient forms blurring into shadow as if they were ghosts, as the sky grew darker.

There was only a single car in the driveway along the side entrance to the house. I parked behind it. A young man materialized out of the shadows of the house and walked toward me as I got out of my car. He was tall and solidly built, with cropped blond hair and intelligent blue eyes peering from behind wire-rimmed glasses.

"John?" he asked, extending his hand. "I'm Joshua Warren."

Wearing a long-sleeved checked shirt and neatly pressed black pants, Joshua resembled a real estate agent eager to sell me the old Smith-McDowell house, but he was, in fact, an established paranormal investigator, author, and founder of the League of Energy Materialization and Unexplained Phenomena Research (L.E.M.U.R. for short).

"Glad you could find the place all right," Joshua said.

"Sure, no problem," I said.

Joshua and I had never met before, although we had exchanged numerous e-mails as we set up my visit, so we chatted for a while, waiting for the house manager and the rest of Joshua's team to show up. After only a few minutes, a woman in sandals, jeans, and T-shirt walked over to us. Tammy Walsh manages the Smith-McDowell house on behalf of its owners, the Western North Carolina Historical Association. The house was fully restored and furnished to depict life from 1840, when it was built, through 1900. It was open to the public during daylight hours, but Tammy would unlock it for us that night and allow us to conduct an investigation.

Tammy said that, although she had never experienced anything unusual in the house, there were people who had, including a psychic who received the impression of a little girl and a dog. In addition, Brian Irish, a sensitive and L.E.M.U.R. investigator, had had a mental image during a previous investigation of a black man chained to a wall in one of the mansion's outbuildings.

"Brian does a lot of our photography," Joshua said. "He should be joining us later tonight."

Two young guys walked up the driveway, both of them wearing suits, and I was instantly reminded that I was in the South; where else but in the South would ghosthunters show up for an investigation wearing suits? In real life, lanky Micah Hanks was a radio producer and musician, and bushy-haired Matt Hixon was in a rock band preparing to go on tour. It didn't take them long to shed their coats, but they never shed their polite southern manners and friendliness.

Before going inside the house, Joshua and I walked around to the front where I took some photos. The tall white columns and rails of the verandah on each level of the house gleamed in the failing light as if they were bone. A yellow light glimmered behind the door on the second floor that led out to the verandah, almost as if some unseen person was expecting us and had lit a light for us to find our way. We rejoined the others and went inside for a quick tour of the house led by Tammy.

"We've been here before," Joshua said, "a few times, but it's always a good idea to walk around again and see what's new or what's been changed."

"What happened those other times?" I asked.

"We detected some areas of unusual electromagnetic activity," Joshua said, "and you already know about Brian's impression. We've been collecting data here, building a file."

Tammy led us across the wide center hall to a front parlor. A high-backed couch and upholstered chair sat before the fireplace. Tea was being served to no one from a silver tea service set upon a small table before the couch. An old case clock stood on the white-painted mantel. A Confederate officer's sword in its scabbard leaned against the mantel. Beside the fireplace stood a headless mannequin, wearing a long white gown, perhaps a bridal gown.

"We recorded some activity in this room the last time we were here," Joshua said. "We'll give it a try later."

Tammy gave us a brief history of the house and its occupants through the years as we roamed its various rooms. I had been in a countless number of old houses before this one, and each time I felt myself transported in time. I felt the same way in the Smith-McDowell house. It was impossible to view clothes, furniture, and personal effects such as framed photos, favorite toys, diaries—and yes, even military memorabilia—without feeling some visceral attachment, some kinship to those people who had gone before. Perhaps that's what ghosts are really all about, I thought. Nothing more than our own psychological and emotional empathy for those forgotten folks, something we conjured up in our minds. On the other hand, some paranormal researchers would say that it was exactly that psychic link, the energy imbued within it that created rather than conjured ghosts. To them, it was simply a matter of which came first: the ghost chicken or the ghost egg.

Inside, the house was growing dim, because we had decided not to turn on any lights as we performed our investigation, but to work in the natural darkness of the mansion. Tammy concluded our tour at the vestibule to the side entrance and left us, agreeing to return later to lock up behind us once we had finished our work.

Leaving the door open to admit more light, the four of us sat on the floor in the vestibule as Joshua unpacked the equipment. When he was just a boy, Joshua had made the acquaintance of Charles Yost, a

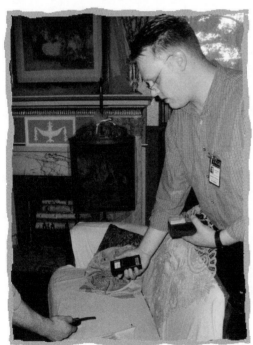

Joshua Warren uses an EMF meter at the Smith-McDowell house.

Courtesy of John Kachuba.

scientist working with the National Aeronautics and Space Administration (NASA), and an unlikely mentor-student relationship developed between them. Joshua's own Tom Swiftian intellect was stimulated by this partnering, and the pile of equipment he assembled on the floor was evidence of his passion for all things electronic. Electromagnetic frequency monitors, remote digital thermometers, Geiger counters, digital voice recorders, night-vision scopes, digital cameras and camcorders with infrared capacities, and a bunch of other stuff were passed around among us while Joshua briefed us on how they were to be used. I didn't remember a thing. Luckily, the other three knew what they were doing.

We began with the EMF meters, which are designed to record the frequencies of electromagnetic radiation. They will record electric outlets, microwaves, TVs, and other electrical appliances, but many paranormal researchers also believe they can detect the presence of ghosts, themselves creatures of energy. The team had a few different types of EMF meters, so as we explored the house we produced a cacophony of squeaks, buzzes, and beeps, not unlike a forest full of cicadas loony on moonshine. Sure enough, as in their last investigation, the parlor seemed to be generating some unusual activity. Both Joshua's and Micah's meters showed high frequencies of electromagnetic energy when they were pointed at the couch. Was a ghost sitting right there before us?

We continued our exploration of the house, the meters spiking every now and then, but the parlor seemed to be the main focus of activity. Brian Irish had arrived and set up a camcorder on a tripod in the doorway of the parlor. I stood beside him, watching through the camera the greenish-colored images of Joshua, Matt, and Micah where they sat on the floor. An EMF meter and voice recorder sat on the floor in front of them. Joshua spoke up and invited any presence that might be in the house to make itself known to us. I admired his direct approach, although no spirit took advantage of it.

Three of us repeated the experiment in the old summer kitchen located in the basement of the house, an area in which a psychic had detected supernatural entities. Joshua, Brian, and I took some EMF readings in the kitchen itself, which had a stone floor and brick walls and was cool and completely dark without our flashlights to show the way. A large wooden table in front of the hearth was set with antique cooking pots and utensils, crockery, and dinnerware. A low doorway in the corner of the room led into a small alcove that once served as a cistern. We decided to set up there for a few minutes.

Brian held the camcorder while Joshua stood beside him, and I stood on Brian's other side, near the doorway of the room. Then we turned off the flashlights and were instantly plunged into complete and utter darkness. The only thing I could see was the tiny red light from Brian's camera glowing in the darkness as though a demon's eye.

I jumped when Joshua spoke aloud in the little room.

"If there is anyone here who would like to make his presence known to us," he said, "we invite you to make contact with us. We are not here to harm you in any way. We would only like to know if you are here." It was strange hearing his voice emanating from the darkness without being able to see him. Eerie, as well. "If you are here," Joshua continued, "give us some sign. Speak to us if you can, but if you are not able to speak, then leave us a sign. Touch one of us, if you wish."

What? I thought. Touch us? Are you out of your mind?

Joshua stopped talking and waited. I could feel my heart thumping in my chest. It seemed that the hairs on my arm were tingling as I anticipated some spectral fondling. The light on Brian's camera glowed.

Matt Hixon and Micah Hanks investigating the Smith-McDowell house.
Courtesy of John Kachuba.

Nothing else was visible. There was no sound. We stood there for hours, I was certain, although it was truly only minutes.

"Are you getting anything, Brian?" Joshua said.

"No," said Brian.

"How about you, John?" asked Joshua.

"Nothing here, either," I said.

Joshua once again invited the ghosts to make themselves known to us, but they were shy and stayed away. We switched our flashlights back on and made our way upstairs.

While Micah and Matt were investigating the second floor of the house, the three of us went outside to the outbuilding where Brian had sensed the presence of a black man chained to the wall. It was a small, brick structure that may once have been used as the slave quarters. The bottom level had a solid door and one single window set in one wall. The top floor of the building was separate from the lower and could only be accessed from an exterior staircase. We had keys for the lower level and unlocked the door. We stepped inside. The single room had a low ceiling with exposed beams. Other than an old workbench pushed up against the wall and a few odd pieces of rusted machinery scattered upon it, the room was empty. The EMF meters did not detect anything unusual in the room, nor did my digital camera.

Still, Brian's memory of an imprisoned man would not leave him alone. He ran his fingers over the rough brick wall. He found some holes in the wall that he believed were spaced in such a way that they could have been used to secure a set of manacles. "I can still see him there, plain as day," Brian said.

We left the room and locked the door behind us.

It was a little past midnight when Tammy returned. We gathered up our gear and exited the house. Micah and Matt drove off, and as I stood in the driveway with Tammy and Joshua, I asked him if he had gotten anything out of the investigation.

"Yes," he said, "I think so."

We didn't have anything unusual happen to us, I thought, in the sense that chairs didn't move across the room by themselves, lights didn't flicker on and off, we didn't hear any ghostly moans or footsteps, and we certainly didn't see a ghost. So, what had we gotten?

"Each time we come to the house and do an investigation, we get a little more data," Joshua said. "This time we got some high EMF readings. All that goes into the file we're building. Sometimes it takes a long time, a lot of data, before you can say what's going on at a particular location. But we're getting there."

That's the way it is with the paranormal. Sometimes you're instantly surprised, but more often than not you're putting in the time and gathering the evidence. Sometimes patience is the most essential tool in a ghosthunter's toolbox.

CHAPTER 4

TOM SWIFT, GHOSTHUNTER

It was 3 a.m. and I was sitting on a couch in a tiny little house deep in the woods of North Carolina with a guy I'd known for only a few hours who, in the previous 20 minutes, had consumed more Kentucky bourbon than I could drink in a year, my right hand enclosed inside a metal box, about to be zapped with 30,000 volts of electricity.

And to think I gave up a career in podiatry.

"Did I say 30,000 volts?" Joshua Warren asked, raising his glass to me in what I hoped was not a farewell salute. "Could be 60 maybe, I don't remember. You'll be fine," he said.

He pushed a button on some kind of electronic box that was attached to mine by wires, I heard a click, and that was it. I was still alive. A few minutes later, he pulled a Polaroid photo out of the box and I watched as a thin circle of glowing white light surrounded by a corona of deep blue developed on the otherwise black photo. The whorls and ridges of my index finger materialized within the circle and there it was: a Kirlian photo of my finger.

Kirlian photography was born in 1939 when Semyon Kirlian discovered, quite by accident, that when an object on a photographic plate is subjected to a high-voltage electric field, an image is created on the plate. Paranormal researchers believe that the halo or corona produced around the image is the physical manifestation of the spiritual aura, or "life force," which they believe surrounds every living thing. Further, some believe that the appearance of the corona can be used as a medical diagnostic tool. In my case, the index finger of my right hand was photographed, and the strong, consistent blue corona outlining my fingertip indicates that my colon and nervous system are healthy and sound. Kirlian photography is not without its detractors, of course, but

Joshua Warren, founder of L.E.M.U.R.
Courtesy of John Kachuba.

it does represent an attempt to apply science to the supernatural, and that is exactly what Joshua Warren is all about.

"I am not a religious person," he said. "I am not dogmatic in the least."

Joshua Warren is an internationally recognized expert on paranormal research and the founder of L.E.M.U.R. (League of Energy Materialization and Unexplained Phenomena Research); the author of *How to Hunt Ghosts* and several other books about ghosts—the first of which was published when he was 13 years old; the host of the radio program

Speaking of Strange; president of Shadowbox Enterprises, LLC, his multimedia production company; an international award-winning filmmaker, working on such films as Patch Adams, Sinkhole, and Paradise Falls; a former columnist for the *Asheville Citizen-Times*; and a leader of expeditions to paranormal sites around the world.

Not bad for a 28-year-old.

But it is for Joshua's expertise as a paranormal investigator that I had come to Asheville, North Carolina. Only a few hours before my finger's debut as a model of Kirlian photography, Joshua and I had conducted an investigation of the Smith-McDowell House, an Asheville antebellum mansion built around 1840 (which you read about in Chapter 3). L.E.M.U.R. team members Micah Hanks, Matt Hixon, and Brian Irish joined us there. Nothing spectacular happened after hours of wandering around in the dark, but Joshua's team collected more data in their ongoing investigation of the mansion.

Afterwards, we all hoisted a few at Barley's, a local bar and restaurant that had also been the site of Asheville's largest mass murder and was purportedly haunted; it's difficult to elude ghosts in Asheville. The next thing I knew, I was driving through dark country lanes, following Joshua's white Monte Carlo to his house. He wanted to show me a History Channel video of his team investigating the North Carolina state capitol building. We watched his team members prowling around the capitol rotunda with the volume turned down low so as not to wake his girlfriend, Lauren, asleep in the next room.

I was having some trouble staying awake, but Joshua said that he's a night owl, so I pushed on and asked him how he became so interested in the scientific approach to the paranormal. He attributes much of his interest to Charles Yost, an engineer who worked for many years with the National Aeronautics and Space Administration, most notably on several Apollo projects, before retiring and starting up his own research laboratory. Joshua says that he first met Charles when the engineer was invited to speak at Joshua's middle school and his teacher introduced them: "Charles was extraordinarily generous with his time and guided me through the process of building my first Tesla coil. I actually hounded him excessively on the telephone about each little step because I didn't want to electrocute myself. He was incredibly patient and he always had that pure sense of spreading knowledge. After that, he realized how serious I was because I was following through on my own and building these devices and he started inviting me to his laboratories to participate in different experiments."

Joshua worked with Charles for several years, until the engineer passed away in 2005. He must have been a star pupil because I could only barely understand our conversation, much of it studded with words such as capacitator, electrostatics, and plasmas—all from Joshua—as I responded with sleep, puppy, and swizzle stick. There is no doubt in my benumbed mind that Joshua was the most intelligent and most articulate paranormal researcher I had ever met.

His experiences with Charles inspired Joshua to create L.E.M.U.R.: "We look at the possible connection between energy, how it manifests in our physical world, and what people describe as paranormal or unexplainable. After we get the data, we take it to the big experts, the Ph.D.s, the universities, and let them take a look at it and give us their opinions. We've been fortunate enough to have worked with scientists from the Oak Ridge National Laboratory and other experts."

The video had run its course and now the television was showing us "snow." The electronic hissing emanating from the screen ties in nicely with Joshua's lecture.

"So, paranormal events are all about electrical discharges," I said. "A ghost is simply a bundle of electricity?"

Joshua poured himself another glass of bourbon from a huge bottle sitting on the coffee table between us.

"When I use the word ghost I always use a very specific definition," he explained. "It's important to do that when you're trying to understand it scientifically and systematically, because so many people mean so many different things when they use the word ghost. For me, a ghost is some paranormal aspect of the physical form and/or mental presence that appears to exist apart from the original physical form."

"Appears?"

"The word appears is very important because that means, in some cases, the experience of seeing a ghost may be something we cannot scientifically differentiate from hallucination. It can be a completely subjective experience, so therefore, ghosts are real at the very least in terms of a human experience. What we are most interested in is figuring out what objective external elements might be there at the time this subjective experience occurred, or possibly triggered the experience as well."

"How can you match that subjective experience with the objective experience, if there is one?" I asked, surprised that my tongue could still work at this late hour.

"We can't nail down the exact cause and effect. You need a laboratory setting to do that, and these things happen under so many variables that we don't understand how to put it all in a laboratory yet. That's why it's so mysterious. That's why we need this very accurate data base in order to begin looking for the patterns and correlations that will allow us to develop a testable hypothesis and actually make some headway in solving some of these mysteries to some degree."

Not only do I admit to being an ignoramus, but I was a sleepy one as well. It was apparent to me that Joshua can go on for hours without so much as a single yawn, but I can't. I've got almost 30 years on him, and it was 4:30 in the morning.

"This is great stuff, Joshua," I said, "but I've got to get some sleep. Can we finish this tomorrow?"

We agreed to meet the following evening at the Grove Park Inn. I said goodnight, drove through deserted streets to my hotel, and stumbled into bed at 5 a.m.

The next evening I met Joshua, his girlfriend, Lauren, and some of the other L.E.M.U.R. guys in the soaring lobby of the venerable old Grove Park Resort Inn & Spa, built in 1913. The place is huge, all granite and wooden beams, and sprawls across a ridge with gorgeous views of Asheville and the Blue Ridge Mountains. Through the years, the inn has played host to many famous personalities, from politicians to sports figures, entertainers to artists. F. Scott Fitzgerald was one frequent guest, using the inn as his home while he visited his wife Zelda, confined to a mental hospital nearby.

The Grove Park has special meaning to Joshua Warren as well. In 1995, he was hired by the inn to investigate the appearances of the Pink Lady, a ghostly young woman wearing a pink dress who apparently fell, or perhaps was pushed, to her death from a fifth-floor walkway over-looking the Palm Court of the inn. It is said that her spirit still haunts Room 545, and many people through the years have reported seeing her. Joshua founded L.E.M.U.R. as a result of his investigation at the inn.

While the rest of the group remained in the lobby, Joshua took me on a tour of the inn. We walked to the wing haunted by the Pink Lady and up to the fifth floor. There was no one else around, and the hallway outside Room 545 was hushed and still.

"No one knows who she was," Joshua said. "Some say she may have been a prostitute, or the girlfriend of some married politician, who may have been killed to keep her quiet. Or it could have been an accident."

The wall overlooking the atrium was not as high as I would have liked it to be, and I could see how a person, perhaps drunk, could eas-ily topple over the rail. I looked down at the stone floor far below. Yep, that would do it, I thought.

Joshua also told me about F. Scott Fitzgerald and the time he shot a few rounds from a pistol into the floor of his room—drunk, of course—and it took some persuasion from the inn staff to pry the gun away from him.

We rejoined the others, and the entire group walked outside to the huge stone terrace. It was a warm July night and the lights of Asheville were just starting to come on in the dusk. We sat around a table, enjoy-ing the view and the fresh air.

I picked up the conversation from where we left off the night before and asked Joshua to tell me about the most unusual experience he has ever witnessed. He told me about an investigation he conducted at a house believed to have poltergeist activity. Many researchers believe that poltergeist are not ghosts, but are in fact the manifestations of energy caused by a living person in the house, albeit unconsciously. Joshua told me that he had set an EMF meter that weighed about a pound on a chair. It sat there for a while, then, as the woman who lived in the house entered the room, the meter fell forward on its face, and then flipped up on its side—a seemingly impossible maneuver. Joshua was lucky enough to have caught the event on videotape, and he explains it as poltergeist activity caused by the woman.

"Have you ever seen a ghost?" I asked.

He told me about a young woman who called him up one morning and said that she had left her house in terror and that she was not going back until her resident ghost could be cleared out. She explained to Joshua that shortly after she had moved in, she began seeing a "man" in her house:

"She was open-minded enough to realize there must be a ghost in her house. She was a bit unsettled and unnerved at first, but it didn't seem to be harming her or even cognizant of her. So, she wasn't extremely traumatized by it at first. It wasn't until this thing started manifesting in her bedroom at night that she started getting scared. Finally, she woke up at 4:30 that morning and this thing was in the bed with her. That's when she said, 'I'm getting the hell out of here and I'm not coming back unless this can be removed.'"

"And you got rid of it?"

"I made it clear to her, as I do often, that I'm not an exorcist, I'm not a ghostbuster. I'm simply there to document whatever is or is not happening and then try to understand it."

Joshua made a visit to the woman's house, but didn't find anything unusual to measure or record. Knowing how rare these kinds of events are and that the odds against something happening to him on a single visit were very high, he set up a second visit.

"On the second occasion," Joshua continued, "I was up in the attic of the house with another researcher. We were about to leave and the other researcher said, 'Josh! Look!' I turned around, and he was just a few feet away from me, and right there between us was this bluish-gray mist, swirling in the air. Right between us. The funny thing is that you would expect us to look at it and say, 'Wow! At long last, a ghost has finally visited me!' but we didn't. We actually looked at it like, I guess, cavemen looking at fire for the first time, flipping through the filing cabinets in our brains thinking, 'Hmm, what could this be? What's the conventional explanation for this?'

"Then it occurred to me, I need to take a picture. I was able to photograph it, which showed that it was an objective manifestation and not just a mutual hallucination we were having. It was there long enough for us to reach out and touch it, and during that period of time I got that icy, electrostatic kind of feeling where the hairs on your knuckles stand up. I would say it was there maybe a total of 20 seconds, which is actually a long time. It did not disperse the way smoke would. Instead, it just dimmed and vanished."

I was impressed by his cool and measured response to an event that would have had me changing my underwear, and I told him that. Joshua smiled and the blue eyes behind the wire-rimmed glasses twinkled. He reminded me that he is a researcher with a sound scientific approach to the paranormal.

"I cannot say that was the spirit of a dead person," he said. "All I can say is that I don't know what it was, but if you place it in proper context with the experiences the woman was having, and add all the other readings we were getting, then it matches my definition of a ghost."

Even stone-cold sober, my mind no longer clouded by lack of sleep, I couldn't find an argument with him.

CHAPTER 5

GHOSTS FOR SALE

Help!!!! We had a house built on this property that used to be occupied by an elderly gentleman that passed away. Now the very first day we had a house built here the little people of spirit have come in and taken things out of their place and in a couple of days or so they return them. One day I was working late on computer and I felt a strange energy. I turned around and saw ethereal figures of children sitting on floor around me. There was a rocking chair and about four children. Somtimes during the daytime I will hear a crash in the kitchen. Usually I go and something has either jumped off the counter or jumped out of the dish rack and bounced to the floor. This is a bit frightening to say the least. I tried contacting people who supposedly know about this sort of thing and I got no response. I even called the paranormal foundation in southern California and left messages in the past. Now I am at my wit's end. I can't stand it when things disappear on me and then return several days later in the same spot that I left them. Last week it was my thermos and some cutting boards. Saturday they were right there in the cabinet where I had them. Last night I was writing one of these and knowing I had to play a gig today my snare drum disappeared...so husband and I pulled this house apart looking for it. Guess what? This morning when I got up it was right in front of my nose in the way of the computer.

Anyway, they need a new home. I am not fooling around. I need to find them a new home b4 i really go nuts. All monies from this auction will be used to start drum circles for senior citizens of Orange County.

I stumbled across this mangled announcement on eBay when I plugged the word ghost into the search box on the Internet. Really, I was only messing around, not expecting to find anything for sale under that rubric other than the Patrick Swayze and Demi Moore movie by that name. (Even though I found a VHS version of the movie for only 99 cents with less than one hour remaining in the auction, I exercised some self-restraint and passed.) But I could not resist stopping at the page that advertised "POLTERGEISTS...THIS IS NOT A JOKE THEY NEED NEW HOME."

I was already reaching for my checkbook.

The name "poltergeist" comes from the German language and translates as "noisy spirit." Traditionally, poltergeists are the spirits that pound on your walls, rap on your windows, throw your china and glassware around the house, jostle your bed while you're sleeping in it, knock over lamps, start small fires in your house, and generally create a lot of mayhem and confusion. They can be a real pain in the neck.

Still, I thought it might be fun to have them around. After all, I was only renting my apartment.

I immediately e-mailed the seller, a woman named Stephanie who lived in Anaheim, California, to get more information. You would think that I would have had some suspicions about the sale, because Anaheim is the home of Disneyland, but no, I did not. Stephanie was for real, it turns out, and I was too late. She had sold her poltergeists.

Well, not quite.

The opening bid for the poltergeists—and I never was able to find out exactly how many of them there were—was one cent. That was also the winning bid, and it seemed reasonable to me, even if Stephanie was selling them by the pound. I was disappointed that I had missed the auction, especially because she had promised to ship the poltergeists in a pretty shopping bag with colored soft tissue paper so they wouldn't have a bumpy landing (her words).

Stephanie told me that she began to have second thoughts about selling her poltergeists, because she didn't know whether or not she could trust the new owner to properly care for them. I didn't know what she meant. Giving them shots? Getting them spayed? In any case, she told the winning bidder to throw his penny into a body of water and to concentrate on the poltergeists finding their way back to their true home.

I thought maybe she'd watched too many Wizard of Oz reruns.

My checkbook was still lying open on my desk, so I continued to browse eBay and discovered a paranormal shopping mall that I would never have believed existed had I not seen it for myself. Here's a partial list of some of the items I found for sale, along with their opening bids:

*   Dead grandfather's haunted fedora—$1
*   Dead golden retriever's haunted stainless steel dog bowl - $200 (owner states that the bowl would be suitable for use by any other pet or pet ghost)
*   Dead grandmother's haunted lamp—$25
*   Haunted, possessed teddy bear—$25 (with free shipping)
*   Dead grandfather's dead dog Bosley's haunted, black studded leather collar—99¢ (owner states collar would be perfect for any pet or someone wanting the "punk rock" look)
*   Dead grandmother's haunted rhinestone earrings—99¢ (owner states he has tried to give the earrings away on numerous occasions, but they always find their way back home)
*   Real ghost in a jar—$10
*   Haunted clown doll complete with ghost of an 8-year-old girl—$6.50
*   Antique child's rocker with ghost boy—$51

And my all-time favorite:

*   Ghost of mother-in-law from Hell—99¢

This is exactly how the posting for the hellish mother-in-law read:

My mother-in-law hated me! She criticized everything I did. I could do nothing to please her. I married her "baby" and she never forgave me for taking him away from her. Now that she is dead, she has come back to haunt me. She won't leave me alone. She re-seasons the food I am cooking and ruins it. She adjusts the dials on the stove so that I burn everything or it boils over onto the floor or turns the oven off and the food is not done on time. She unmakes the beds and scatters dust over everything so that my husband thinks I sit around and eat bon bons all day instead of cleaning the house and I think she is unwrapping the Christmas presents! With Christmas coming, I need to be rid of her so that she won't spoil it. Please help before I go mad! I will send you her toothbrush, hair curlers and showercap so that she will go with the package. I will use the money from the auction to redecorate her room and put flowers on her grave. I AM NOT RESPONSIBLE FOR HER AFTER SHE IS PACKED AND MAILED TO HER NEW OWNER! (I really think that casino that bought the Grampa Ghost should buy this Great Great Grandmother Ghost. Maybe they could get together and be happy!) I should also mention that she is 100% CAJUN and liked her food very spicy so don't blame me if she uses a lot of cayenne! She was always a peach around other people so she will probably be very well behaved and you will love her. Absolutely no returns or refunds!

Sunday Dec 12, 2004.... Help!!!!!!!!!!!!! She is at it again. Today, while the DISH SAT. REPAIR MAN WAS WATCHING, I was taking a batch of hot homemade oatmeal raisin cookies (her favorite!) out of the oven, I placed the cookie sheet on top of the range and turned around and it flipped off the range and turned upside down on the rug in front of the oven! All landed on the rug...not a crumb on the floor. The dish guy was through with his repairs and I had pulled this web site up to show him and he was sitting in front of the computer reading it when it happened and he said "I am a witness to that!!" Please Help!!!!! I am going out of my mind!

I must admit I could see her point, but I just could not will myself to purchase someone's used toothbrush, hair curlers, and shower cap, haunted or not. I put away my checkbook.

Many of the descriptions that accompanied these haunted items made me pause to consider what was really going on. Were these items haunted, really? The haunted, possessed teddy bear on the list was one such item. The owner stated that he woke to hear a woman's voice saying it was 2 o'clock in the morning, and that he saw a woman in a "see-through white gown" walking through the house. I noted that it was the gown that was "see-through" and not the woman. Maybe it's just me, but I'd welcome such a haunting anytime.

And what about the haunted clown doll, complete with ghost of an 8-year-old girl? The owner, who collects dolls and other knick-knacks, said that she meticulously researched every doll she bought by sending it to the "department of parapsychology at our university." That's proof enough for me, but I was concerned by the fact that she let her own daughter—who I had every reason to believe was a flesh-and-blood little girl—play with the haunted doll and its attached ghost. What was she thinking?

Still, all this phantom merchandising got me wondering if there wasn't a penny or two to be made here. A lot of people were selling haunted items, and I was sure they had stumbled into a virtual gold mine. I started thinking about what haunted, or possessed (I wasn't being choosy) things I had lying around the house that I could sell.

There was the ghost in my haunted Maytag clothes dryer that always stole one sock from every pair. Maybe start the bidding at $100.

There was the little haunted glass-topped end table that flipped coffee mugs and plates onto the floor if they were placed too near the edge. $15?

What about my haunted bicycle, whose tires would mysteriously deflate after only a few months? Surely, that was worth a couple hundred bucks. I could even offer free shipping, because the ghost could simply pedal himself to his new owner.

Then I thought of the perfect eBay item: my Ghosthuntermobile. Oh, sure, to most people the car was simply a dented and rusted-out 1987 Buick Skyhawk, but I had inherited it from my deceased father-in-law. I'm not saying that Cliff's spirit was still in the car, but I did visit more than 70 haunted locations in that car as I researched my books. Something must have attached itself to the car somewhere along the line. But the main selling point, at least to my mind, was that I had had the car painted all over with ghosts, demons, and other spooky images to help advertise my books—a billboard on wheels, courtesy of Ohio University art instructor Barrett Skrypeck and friends. Now, who wouldn't want such a vehicle? So, don't be surprised if you find that car listed on eBay: IT IS A FOR-REAL GHOSTHUNTERMOBILE. THIS IS NO JOKE.

Chapter 6

The Demonologist

DavConsidine is a thin, wiry guy neatly dressed in a black polo shirt and pressed tan pants. He sports a wispy moustache and goatee, his hair conservatively cut. Beneath his black ball cap—*The Amityville Horror* embroidered in scarlet across the front—his blue eyes are friendly, candid. He looks to be your typical lay religious demonologist.

David Considine, founder of Phantasm Psychic Research.
Courtesy of John Kachuba.

Which he is.

We were sitting in a crowded, tiny office above a store in a Connecticut coastal town. The warm summer night swarmed outside, but the heavy black curtains over the windows keep it at bay. (David asked me not to reveal the name of the town because he doesn't want his office besieged by weirdoes, kooks, and occultists who may have an unhealthy interest in his activities.)

The Office of Phantasm Psychic Research (PPR) is unlike any other office I have ever seen. It's little more than an elongated closet, but it's crammed with a weird and horrific collection of souvenirs and mementos gathered from PPR's work across the country. At one end, beside an innocuous table, upon which stands a coffeemaker and plate of Oreo cookies, there is a large square cabinet draped in black cloth. A cross is mounted above the cabinet in which David tells me he keeps under lock and key "dangerous" objects taken from haunted sites or used in satanic rituals. A monitor above the cabinet is showing a tape of people dressed in green Druid-styled cloaks running around in the woods; David uses a remote control from where he sits behind a miniature desk at the other side of the room to turn off the video. Assembled near the monitor and on shelves above it are items that, to me, resemble leftovers from a paranormal yard sale: a large statue of St. Michael the Archangel; a black coiled serpent that David says is a tulpa, a representation of a snake made from blood and feces and other profane stuff that conjured up the real thing upon a sleeping woman's chest; a religious statue that had been defiled by occultists with human waste, now cleaned and kept under a bell jar; a large, amber candle set in a tall candlestick holder; and pieces of a wooden chair broken by a possessed woman during her exorcism.

A few metal folding chairs were placed along one wall, and I was seated in one next to David's desk. In the corner was a tall bookcase loaded with candles, replicas of human skulls, devil masks, an unopened bottle of Drambuie, pentacle pendants on chains, an ankh, a Santeria ritual plate complete with a small animal skull and dead puffer fish fully puffed, and an animated, talking ghost doll.

My face must have registered some surprise because David explained that most of the items on the shelves are used as teaching aids for students enrolled in his ghosthunting and paranormal classes.

"Actually, I was wondering about the ghost doll," I said.

"A joke gift from a friend," David explained, placing the doll on his desk and switching it on. "It's important to have a sense of humor in this work." Meanwhile, the little ghost shivered and moaned.

There are two humorous signs hanging on the walls, one that reads "Ghost Crossing," and the other that says "Ghost Stories Told Here." They share wall space with a fake goat's head and candleholder, assorted crosses, a movie poster from *The Exorcist*, photos of ghosts taken on investigations, pictures of celebrities of the paranormal world, and photos of David posing with various clergymen who are colleagues in his work as a demonologist.

This whole demonologist thing throws me, even as I sat talking with David and the other members of his team, who were filtering in for the interview. Other than my discussions through the years with Ed and Lorraine Warren, the king and queen of demonology, no other ghost investigator has spoken about the connection between the diabolical and ghosts. David Considine and PPR first came to my attention when I read about him cleansing a California house of its demons by performing a suffumagation, which David later explains as something of a religious fumigation, using frankincense, myrrh, and other incenses. Saint Terminix? My curiosity was piqued.

From the moment I stepped into the office, it was obvious that David is deadly serious about his work, but excited as well. He took out a stack of photos from his desk and began showing me pictures of ghosts—misty streaks and swirls, orbs of light—taken in homes and cemeteries. There are photos of actual exorcisms, too, with the faces of the possessed blurred to protect their privacy. In one, a little possessed girl sits on a couch between two women. In the next photo, taken, David said, at the exact moment of the girl's exorcism, a large black mist obscures the left side of the photo. The demon being cast out, David said.

"I'm confused," I said, handing the photo back to him. "What exactly does PPR do?"

"The group originally started as a research group but turned into a group that helps people," David said. "We handle all kinds of cases: poltergeists; common, traditional hauntings; demonic infestations; possessions; occultic-type crimes; occult activity. No matter what it is, we try to find a way to handle it. Simply put, we aid people who are having problems with the supernatural, problems with the preternatural."

I had heard those terms before in my talks with the Warrens. It was no surprise that David repeated them, because for 14 years he had trained under the Warrens and had been one of their chief researchers. By supernatural these researchers mean activity caused by any force or agent that is not part of the physical, earthly realm. By preternatural, they mean phenomena caused by inhuman spirits considered possessed of a negative, diabolical intelligence.

David made it clear that PPR is not only prepared to investigate the average Casper the Friendly Ghost type of haunting, but also packs enough psychic heat to take on the full-blown, screaming, ranting, raving spirits seen in *The Exorcist*. No other group I had worked with could make that claim. Since David founded PPR in 1994 the group had investigated hundred of hauntings across the country and in Canada, and has been involved in scores of exorcisms.

"I work from the perspective of a lay religious demonologist," David said, "meaning I am not a man of the cloth, but was taught by a lay religious demonologist, Ed Warren, and by different bishops and priests who are themselves theologians and have been involved in this field a lot longer than I have been."

He took a letter of recommendation out of the desk drawer and handed it to me. It states that David is, as he says, a lay religious demonologist, fully trained in demonology. A Catholic bishop, one of several clergymen he enlists to actually perform the exorcism, has signed the document.

"I use this letter, and letters from families we have helped in the past, with new people seeking our help so that they know I'm fully trained in this field."

"And that convinces them to allow you to investigate?" I asked.

"That, and the fact that we do whatever we can to protect their privacy. We don't let any other people know what we're doing. We generally arrive under cloak of night."

As I handed the letter back to David, Barbara Considine, sitting beside me, spoke up. A woman about my own age, she wore a baby blue crocheted vest over a blouse and black slacks, and had short, dark hair and glasses. She looked to be a mom, and indeed, she is David's mother.

"It's like social work," she said. "You go into a house and people tell you things they would never tell a stranger. It amazes me how they open up, but they have to because in order for us to help them, we have to know everything that's going on before we can make a decision. You really have to know what you're doing. It can be a dangerous business."

David picked up on his mother's words and said, "Sometimes you can run into situations that can get out of control. I've been in just about every situation you can think of, from going into a house that was completely dilapidated, to having a homeowner point a gun at me, to being screamed at by a family member who's gone out of control, to being slammed up against a wall during a possession."

I had studied enough about demonic possession to know that it doesn't always present itself in as gruesome a form as shown in the movie *The Exorcist*. Your head doesn't have to revolve completely around in order to be possessed, although it does create an awesome effect if you can do it.

As if she had read my mind—and who knows, maybe she had—Barbie Heid, another of the PPR investigators, told me about an experience she had with a possessed man.

She explained to me that it is the group's policy to always have at least one team member stay with each of the family members during a possession investigation. Barbie said that she was sitting with the father of the family in his kitchen, talking and drinking their way through two large pots of coffee.

"During the night his whole personality changed," Barbie said. "He's a big guy, well over 6 feet, and he's sobbing on my shoulder, saying 'I can't protect my family and kids. I don't know what to do,'" and Barbie drew out that last word in such a plaintive keening as she sat on the edge of her chair, that for a moment, I felt as though I was in that house and could see the man sitting across from me. It's unsettling.

"At the end of the night," Barbie continued, holding her coffee cup in two hands upon her lap, "after this influence came over him, his eyes turned into little slits, he got deep, deep crow's feet, deep lines by his jowls. His voice got very gravelly, nasty. I called him by his name and he looked at me as if to say, 'I don't know who you're talking to.' It was amazing."

She added, "Demonic spirits need to hide. They can't be detected."

"The demonic spirit will try to mask itself," David said. "It's called a larva spirit, from the Latin larva, meaning "specter," or "mask." In the larva state, it will not show itself for what it truly is. It may present itself as a ghost—a little girl ghost, let's say. It has patience way beyond human endurance and it waits until the family starts accepting it into its life as that harmless little girl ghost, and then it starts changing. Doors start banging; the little girl ghost is gone now. It never was a little girl. The diabolical works on human recognition and tries to gain a stronghold in the person's family or the family's way of thinking. Once the phenomena starts to occur it has that stronghold necessary to start to destroy that family."

I was making notes while the tape recorder churned on, and I wished I could pause to digest some of the information the group had been throwing at me. Luckily, they're mostly all smokers and were in need of a cigarette break. So while they all went outside to grab a smoke, I had a few moments to review my notes. Barbara Considine, apparently a non-smoker, returned after just a few moments and we talked some more.

Barbara spoke with great conviction about how important the services PPR renders are. She emphasized again the similarities between the group's work and social work. She did not put down the many other paranormal research groups that are combing through cemeteries all across America, but it is obvious that she thinks many of those groups are less professional than PPR, less serious about their work.

David came back before the others.

"Hey, do you know what this is?" he asked, reaching down by the bookcase and retrieving a piece of cardboard maybe 2 feet long by a foot wide. It was a collage of some sort, pictures and words cut out from magazines and glued to the board. There was a glare on the board from the overhead lights and I reached out a hand to adjust it.

David snatched it out of my reach. "No, you don't want to touch it."

"I don't?"

"Believe me, you don't want to," David said. He tilted the board so I could get a better view, and I noticed that he was holding it with his fingers placed over a St. Michael the Archangel holy card, which was paper-clipped to the board. "Tell me what you see," he said.

There were two unrecognizable figures in the center of the board, a yellow one on the left, a bluish-black one on the right. They had something of the shape of people wrapped in robes, but I wasn't sure. The other pictures glued to the board seemed mundane enough, nothing particularly frightening or weird as far as I could tell. After only a few moments I realized that the cut-out words all had negative connotations. Anger. Revenge. Jealousy. Hatred. I pointed this out to David.

"Right, exactly," he said. "This is a curse board. This one was used to curse someone in a failed relationship. It carries some strong energy. That's why I didn't want you to touch it."

"Okay with me," I said, as he set it down again.

The others had come back into the room, bringing with them the clinging odor of cigarette smoke. I asked David how much of his time is spent on cases of demonic possession compared to the garden-variety ghost hunt.

He took his *Amityville Horror* cap off and placed it dead-center on the desk. "I have six cases that I'm working on right now that may require exorcism."

"Six?"

"In the last three and a half months, I have investigated over two dozen cases of demonic infestation or possession."

"That's amazing," I said. "I had no idea."

He smiled slightly. "The devil's greatest weapon is that no one believes it exists. But I know what can happen. I've seen investigators slammed into walls, thrown down stairs, thrown across rooms. I myself have been psychically gashed. When you have possession, the diabolical wants to single that person out to the point where he has no family, he has no friends, he has no social life, period. It singles him out to the point where he gives up. The ultimate goal of the diabolical is suicide. It wants you to give up your immortal soul."

David's words sounded melodramatic in the little office, but one look at his face and I could see he was not joking. I could make no reply.

CHAPTER 7

THE COFFEE SHOP GHOSTS

As I walked down Main Street in Torrington, Connecticut, I saw Betty Boop standing on the sidewalk outside Chiane's. Ever slutty— but in a cutie-pie sort of way—she was wearing a short, form-fitting red uniform and a little red cap tilted jauntily on her enormous head. She was holding a tray above her head with one hand. A man came out of Chiane's, grabbed Betty around the waist and carried her off into the coffee shop. When I pushed open the door to Chiane's, Betty was already silently standing in a corner, the overhead light reflecting off her scarlet-painted uniform.

Charlie Marczewski was the guy who had manhandled the plastic statue; he was also one of the owners of Chiane's, a coffee/sandwich shop that had been in business for only a little more than a year, but that was apparently haunted by ghosts who had been there a lot longer. At Charlie's request, David Considine's Phantasm Psychic Research team of investigators was scheduled that evening to check out the place. David had invited me to join them.

It was about 7 p.m. on a warm evening in July. Customers came and went, many of them drifting across the street to the Warner Theater, whose neon marquee glowed in the night like a lighthouse. The PPR team had not yet arrived, so I sat with Charlie on barstools at the end of the counter while Diane Persechino, Charlie's business partner and fiancée, tended to the customers.

I didn't mind waiting, because Chiane's was a pleasant place to wait. The shop was long and narrow, with wood floors and a tin ceiling. Old-fashioned ceiling fans cut the air. The walls were painted bright yellow with maroon trim and were hung with original paintings and a collection of ceramic Green Man masks from local artists. A fake fireplace stood against one wall. Behind the counter, an assortment of mugs hung below little brass nametags, bearing the names of regular customers: Al, Joe Q., Blinky.

"I bought those for my regulars and gave them out as Christmas presents last year," Charlie said.

"Have any of your customers seen the ghosts?" I asked.

"One guy came in and sat down at the counter and almost immediately said that we had ghosts, but mostly it's been me and Diane who have seen them," he said. "Diane was the first."

"I heard them before I saw them," Diane said, coming over to where Charlie and I sat. "I was down in the basement and I heard voices from upstairs and furniture being moved across the floor. There hadn't been anyone in the store when I went downstairs, but I called up, 'I'll be right with you.' I kept hearing the chairs being dragged across the floor and the voices. I went upstairs and there was no one there. Nothing was moved. Everything was in its right place. After that incident, I saw a woman standing by the cash register who disappeared, and another time, a figure standing by the front door with its arms folded in front of it."

"I was a little skeptical at first," Charlie said, "because I wasn't seeing anything. But then it happened to me. I was in the kitchen slicing meat. I turned around and there was this male face right up close to me. It quickly receded back and then disappeared. It was smiling.

"There's another one, too," Charlie continued, "that we've both seen. He's kind of a husky guy with big arms, wearing a white shirt. I saw him walking into the kitchen, hunched over. He looked back at me over his shoulder and then he was gone."

"What do you think is going on here?" I asked.

Charlie shook his head. "I don't know, but a lady from Denmark came into our shop not too long ago and told us that she was psychic and that we had ghosts in here. She said that those ceramic masks on the wall were Pagan gods and that they were arranged in a specific order to 'open a window'."

"But didn't you hang them yourself?" I asked.

"The artist did," Charlie said. "This woman also said we were mixing water with fire, because we had a fishbowl on the mantel over the fake fireplace, and that was not a good thing."

"What did you think of all that?"

"I didn't know what to think. She said she was able to get rid of some of them, but that there were too many ghosts for her to handle."

"I think there are still spirits here that need to pass over," Diane added.

"Is that why you called PPR?" I asked.

"My dishwasher told me that his uncle had worked with them," said Charlie. "I didn't want any crazies here, but he told me that they worked in a Christian manner, so that sounded okay."

It was now past 8 p.m. I had been there an hour and no one from PPR had shown up yet. Charlie asked me if I wanted to see the basement, so I followed him downstairs. It was pretty much what I had expected. Dusty. Dingy. There were some storage areas for supplies, some which held only junk, a tiny office, but nothing out of the ordinary.

"Diane was in this office when she heard all the noise from upstairs," Charlie said.

I noticed how muffled sounds were down there, so whatever Diane had heard it must have been loud.

We went back upstairs and I waited for the investigators to arrive, polishing off a bowl of mocha gelato while I waited. Obviously, we had gotten our psychic signals crossed, because when the team finally arrived past 10 o'clock, David said they had been having dinner at a nearby diner and were wondering why I hadn't joined them.

David was accompanied by half a dozen or so team members, but they waited until after the coffee shop closed for the night before dragging in the huge trunks that carried their equipment. Diane left, but Charlie remained for a while to see how the investigation would proceed.

David and John Arel, PPR's technical director, pushed two tables together in the rear of the shop, where they assembled their equipment. John was a tall, middle-aged, bespectacled guy with unruly silvery gray hair and a walrus moustache. He had been with David since the group was first formed and was an electronic whiz. He worked for a security company and was highly inventive when it came to developing new equipment for the group's research. He showed me an extremely sensitive microphone he had put together called Big Ear.

"I tested Big Ear at home, when I first built it," he said. "The microphone was downstairs in my living room and I was on the third floor of the house, behind closed doors in my bedroom, which is on the opposite side of the house. I clapped my hands and Big Ear picked up the sound. There's not much it won't pick up."

It's no wonder the other team members have nicknamed him Mac-Gyver. "Give me a paper clip and a book of matches and I'll come up with something," John said.

I was fascinated as I watched the team unpack their equipment from the trunks. I had never seen so much, well, stuff. John and David

Phantasm's Tricia Arthur checking the monitor at Chiane's.
Courtesy of John Kachuba.

explained some of the electronics to me as they set it all up on the tables. They unpacked two monitors: One would simultaneously display a split-screen image of four quadrants, one for each of the video cameras the other team members were setting up in the shop. The second monitor could be tuned to any single quadrant at will to get a larger view. There was a thermal imager, a little gizmo that, at the click of a button, would take a still picture of whatever was on the monitor at the time and instantly spit it out for closer inspection.

The person who would mostly be responsible for watching the monitors was Tricia Arthur.

"I've got a good eye and I'm quick with the imager," Tricia said.

"She doesn't miss a thing," David added.

Tricia is also sensitive to spirits.

"I can feel things," she said. "I can't talk to them or discern them, but I can feel them. I became aware of my ability when I was six years old. I thought it was normal, I thought everyone could do it."

David and John had lugged a large piece of equipment onto the table and were fiddling with it. It had a round screen with crosshairs and looked to be something out of a World War II submarine movie. A bright green band wobbled and danced in crazy patterns on the screen.

"This is a line analyzer," David said. "It's pretty expensive and very few groups have one. It will detect sound waves and levels far below that of the human voice, which is roughly 3,000 hertz. This thing can record sound at frequencies as low as 300 hertz. By comparing the frequencies with our electronic voice recordings we can tell whether the sound was made by a human voice or not."

As we were talking, the other team members had set up video cameras on tripods, along with microphones, in the basement, in the kitchen, and in two different locations in the upstairs dining room. Barbara Considine, David's mother, was taping all the wires to the floor with duct tape so that none of us would trip over them once the lights were out.

There was a lot of testing of equipment, a lot of adjustments to be made, the inevitable electronic failures that required one stubborn monitor to be replaced by a new one from the van parked outside, and it wasn't until 11:45 that we were ready to go. We turned off the lights and waited.

Contrary to the frenetic ghosthunting experiences depicted in the movie *Ghostbusters*, a real ghosthunt entails a great deal of sitting around waiting for something to happen. Often, the long wait results in nothing. It is not at all uncommon for investigators to conduct several investigations at a location for a period of time, collecting data bit by bit, the tedium every now and then being broken by brief moments of excitement when something truly memorable occurs.

I sat beside Tricia, watching the monitors and the line analyzer. Tricia wore a headset that allowed her to speak with two team members who were in the basement. The rest of the team was stationed in the kitchen, by the camera at the front of the shop, or huddled in front of the bank of electronic gadgetry. Every so often someone would change positions, his flashlight beam moving like a firefly in the dark.

John came over and stood behind the equipment. He said something but, blinded by the glare from the monitors and other equipment, I could not see him when I looked up; I could only hear him. When I replied, I pitched my voice in the direction from where I had heard the seemingly disembodied voice and hoped that I was looking at him.

After a while David slid onto the bench beside me. He and Tricia had a discussion about a spot of light that appeared in one quadrant on the monitor. They didn't believe it was caused by anything paranormal, but it was an obstacle to their view. They tried adjusting the cameras and moving objects they thought might be producing unwanted reflections, but they were never able to figure out what was creating the interference.

"We'll just have to live with it," David said.

We talked a little as we sat there keeping an eye on the equipment, and I asked David how he had become a paranormal investigator. He said that when he was 12 years old he had encountered a ghost.

"I was fishing one day. It was actually later at night, down by a river, and this dark shape came upon me on my left side. It terrified me. I broke my fishing rod, threw down my tackle box, and ran out of there. I went back down there later, but I never saw it again."

David said that after his brush with the paranormal he started reading everything he could get his hands on related to the subject. He begged his parents to take him to a lecture being given by famed ghosthunters Ed and Lorraine Warren, and after the lecture he spoke with Ed.

"I told him I wanted to do what he did," David said. "I was just a teenager, and Ed said to come back in a few years. I continued to read and study and went back to Ed, who took me under his wing and showed me what to do. I worked with Ed and Lorraine for about 14 years as one of their chief researchers, working my way up through the ranks."

We tuned our attention back to the monitors. There wasn't much happening. In the greenish images on the screen we saw everyone sitting quietly at their assigned stations. I shifted my feet beneath the table and leaned closer.

"Wait. What was that?" Tricia said.

"Where?" asked David.

"It was right there," Tricia said, pointing to the quadrant in the lower left quarter of the screen.

I moved forward, tucking me feet beneath my chair.

"There!" said Tricia. "Did you see it?"

"Yes," said David.

"I saw it too," I added. Two globes of shining light moving low on the screen. It took me a few moments to realize that the image being displayed in that quadrant was the area of the shop in which we were sitting.

"Wait a minute," I said, and I deliberately moved my feet under the table. As I did so, bright balls of light danced across the screen. "Oh, crap," I said.

"It's your shoes, isn't it?" David said.

"Yes," I said. "Sorry about that," referring to the reflective strip on the back of each of my tennis shoes that the camera had so ably detected.

For a long time after that false alarm nothing happened. Some of the team members were sipping coffee or soft drinks to keep themselves from falling asleep. I was wide awake, because I had taken a short nap that afternoon to gear up for this all-night investigation. So was Tricia.

"I think we had something then," she suddenly said, speaking into her microphone. "Did you guys get anything?"

The two investigators in the basement answered in the negative.

"What did you see?" I asked. I was looking at the monitors as well but had seen nothing.

"We got some movement," she said.

David returned along with a few other team members. They assembled around the monitor.

"Whoop, there we go again," Tricia said, and someone else said they saw it, too: a little ball of light zipping through the image on the screen. I didn't see it, but some minutes later I did see something vague and indistinct, a small shadow of some kind moving through the darkness of the basement. Several of us saw it.

"What is that?" I asked, but no one answered.

We watched for a while more, but everything was quiet. Whatever it was that we think we had seen in the basement had called it a night. It was now 4:30 in the morning and David decided to do the same. We turned on the lights and began the long process of packing up the equipment. I was talking to Jeff Messenger, who had been one of the guys who spent much of the night in the basement, sometimes alone. Even though a camera had been set up down there he had also been filming with his own camcorder, and now he showed me what the camera had picked up.

"None of this was visible to the naked eye," he said, as he flipped out the little viewer on the side of the camera. "Watch."

The image was small and dark, but suddenly the darkness was broken by a streak of brilliant light that tracked quickly in a descending arc from the top of the picture to the bottom.

"I wonder if that's what we saw on the monitor upstairs," I said.

"Here's another," Jeff said, handing me the camera. This time, a globe of light shot across the bottom of the picture in a straight line, passing from left to right as though it were a paranormal fastball. "Pretty cool, huh?" Jeff said.

After the long night we had just spent at Chiane's, I had to admit, it was very cool indeed.

CHAPTER 8

LICENSE AND REGISTRATION, PLEASE

Grafton, Illinois, is a one-blink kind of town. Blink your eyes once, and you're through it. Graftonites don't have much to occupy their time, and this is especially true of the police department. That's why, on one cold December day, I was pulled over by a member of Grafton's finest—not because I was speeding (I wasn't), or because the car's taillight was out (it wasn't), or because the car was missing a license plate (it wasn't), but simply because I was driving the Ghosthuntermobile, a 1987 Buick Skyhawk, painted all over with ghosts, tombstones, haunted houses, and other paranormal iconography. The cop was curious, if not downright suspicious.

I thought about how cool it would be to be able to whip out some impressive form of identification instead of the standard license and registration, something that would make the officer snap to attention and salute me, maybe even provide me with a flashing-light-and-siren escort through town.

Maybe some document declaring me a Certified Ghosthunter.

Yeah, that would do it.

I was vaguely aware that ghosthunters could obtain some kind of certification that showed they had attained a certain level of expertise in their field. I remembered someone handing me a business card at a conference with the words Certified Paranormal Investigator printed on the card after his name. I didn't think about it much at the time, but later I started wondering what it meant to be certified and hopped on the Internet to see what I could find.

Yes, there were indeed several options available to me if I wanted a nicely printed diploma to hang on my wall. I could become a Registered Ghost Researcher, a Certified Ghost Researcher, a Certified Ghosthunter, or a Certified Paranormal Investigator. (I also found one Massachusetts ghosthunter who said on her website that she was "licensed," although no state offers any kind of license to ghosthunters.) Various individuals and groups offered these pedigrees, and most of them were home-study courses, so I didn't even have to leave the comfort of my decidedly un-haunted home to earn my sheepskin. I did have to write a check, however, in amounts that ranged from $30 for the Michigan Ghost Watchers' Certified Paranormal Investigator course, to $175 for the International Ghost Hunters Society's Certified Paranormal Investigator course. To be fair to the IGHS, I could purchase both the Certified Paranormal Investigator course and the Certified Ghost Researcher course for only $300; they also offered a Certified EVP Researcher course if I wanted to further my paranormal education. Hollow Hill offered a Certified Ghost Hunter course for $149, as did Ghost Chasers International. Ghost Trackers came in at $80 for a similarly titled course, and Sherri Brake-Recco's Ghosthunting 101 was $39. One big difference among these courses was that both Ghost Chaser International and Ghosthunt-ing 101 were conducted in a live classroom setting, rather than at home, and included actual investigations as training methods.

As I read through the information posted by these various groups, I began to realize that getting my certification, if that is what I finally chose to do, wouldn't necessarily be a walk in the park (or cemetery). Michigan Ghost Watchers warned me that I would have to "pass written examination with at least 35 of 40 questions correct" in order to earn their Ghost Hunter Certificate. It was 20 out of 25 questions for the group's Paranormal Investigator Certificate, plus I would have to "do a field investigation and submit a photograph along with a written report."

The question nagging me all along was whether or not these courses and their subsequent certificates made any difference. I had been on several investigations all around the country with paranormal research teams whose members carried no certification of any kind, but who were knowledgeable and competent. Would a certificate have made them any more so? Would a certificate have made their job any easier in some way? Given them access to places they could not normally have visited? Smoothed things over with the police? Earned them a discount at Pizza Hut?

The larger question, of course, was by what authority did these various groups and individuals offer certification? There was no single agency or organization that set standards for these courses or supervised them in any way to ensure quality or consistency. This meant that each course was different from the others, and it would be impossible to predict what you would learn as a student until you had taken the course. In other words, some courses would be valuable, others not so much.

These were all important questions to consider, and I decided the only way to answer them would be to go ahead and try to earn my certification. So, I enrolled in Patti Starr's Ghost Hunting Certification course in Lexington, Kentucky. I chose Patti for several reasons. First, I had spoken with several people who had taken her course and each of them had high praise for her teaching abilities. Second, I had read good reports about her course and her Ghost Chasers International group in several different newspaper articles, and, finally, Patti agreed to allow me to take her course, even though she knew it would be fodder for this chapter. The lady was nothing if not brave.

Patti offers ghosthunting courses through Lexington Community College and also in the offices of her husband Chuck's equestrian art gallery. That's where I was to take the course.

I was the first to arrive that Saturday morning at the low, nondescript brick building that housed both Chuck's business and Patti's Ghost Hunter Shop. I parked my car next to a late-model Buick with license plates that read GHOSTS. A chime sounded as I walked into the lobby. Before I could fully take in the paintings and sculptures of racehorses filling the room, a smiling balding guy with glasses came out to greet me. Chuck Starr was stocky and genial, a few years older than me. He was casually dressed in an electric blue sweater, navy sweatpants and tennis shoes. Chuck led me into a conference room where a long wooden table surrounded by comfortable black leather chairs took up most of the space. The blinds were closed over the windows and bucolic paintings of horse farms hung on the walls. A small TV hooked up to a laptop computer sat on a credenza at one end of the conference table. The table held small stacks of Patti Starr's book, Ghost Hunting in Kentucky and Beyond and, I was happy to see, copies of my book, Ghosthunting Ohio. I knew we would get along just fine.

That feeling was reinforced when Patti entered the room. A lively and energetic woman with a charming Southern accent, Patti greeted me as if we had known each other for years. She wore black slacks and a blue sweater, over which she sported the official Ghost Chasers International vest, a multi-pocketed affair with "Ghost Chasers" embroidered in the back and "Patti" on the front, just above a ghost pin. A watch dangled

Patti Starr in her Ghost Hunter Shop in Lexington, Kentucky.
Courtesy of John Kachuba.

from a D-ring on the vest. Patti is petite with short blond hair neatly coiffed and happy blue eyes behind gold wire-frame glasses. For some reason, I had the pleasant impression of Mrs. Santa Claus when I met Patti—that is, if Mrs. C. lost a lot of weight and spoke with a Charleston, South Carolina, accent.

We didn't get too much time to talk before the other students in this introductory Ghosthunting 101 course began filing in, taking seats around the long table. We all introduced ourselves and told a little about why we were there. Besides me, there were five other students: a middle-aged woman who worked in a haunted hotel and had experienced paranormal activity most of her life; a young married couple, the blond wife possessing a lifelong ability to see ghosts, and the husband, who wore a heavy silver necklace outside his T-shirt, a skeptic; and two bespectacled brothers who had also witnessed paranormal events. One of them, a shy mountain of a man, who was a musician and graphic artist and sported a beard, ponytail, earring, and a stud piercing the flesh below his lower lip, said that he lived in a haunted house, but that he had come to terms with his ghosts. Now he was curious and wanted to learn more about them.

Patti talked a bit about her life, how she had grown up in a strict Baptist environment in the South, and how, despite that upbringing, she had been in the company of ghosts all her life, even as a little girl.

"I'm a haunted person," Patti said. "In my lifetime, I've lived in 35 different places and they've all been haunted. So, it's not the place that's haunted. I attract ghosts." She went on to say that she sees ghosts mostly in the afternoon rather than at night, and that the hours between 2 and 4 p.m. were the best for ghostly visits. She also explained that her abilities were not unique. "We're all psychic in some way. It's God's gift. If we weren't, we wouldn't be able to survive."

She introduced Chuck, her husband of six years, to the group. Chuck was sitting in for only a few minutes because he had his own business to attend to that morning. He admitted that he had not given much though to ghosts until he met Patti and they started dating. At first, he provided logistical support for Patti, but gradually he became more interested in her work, and after a few investigations with her, his initial skepticism began to erode.

"I'm a thorough believer now," Chuck told the students. "There's no way, with all the evidence I've seen, that there can't be ghosts." He spoke about what hunting ghosts has meant to him on a personal level. "This has been the ride of my life," he said. "I've met some great people. Ghost people are the salt of the earth, people you'd invite into your home."

Well, all right then, I was convinced.

Passing out purple folders containing various handouts, Patti formally began the five-hour class. She used a Microsoft PowerPoint presentation to augment her lecture and included photos and videos from past investigations. Patti admitted that ghosthunting was not a science, but said that the proper training—and certification—could make ghost-hunting more "scientific" in its approach. She talked about the 60 or so members of her Ghost Chasers International organization and said, "Every one of our investigators is certified. No other group can say that. When we go on an investigation, we're going there as a scientific group to find out about it."

She said that an investigation should be carried out only by certified team members—no friends, no relatives, no children. I had been on investigations in which all three had been present, and I had to admit, some of those investigations resembled the Three Stooges at Disneyland more than a science project. Patti also banned smoking, alcohol, and drugs—legal or otherwise—on her investigations.

Patti talked about the protocol she had set up for conducting investigations, and I was pleased to hear her emphasis on being respectful of the place and the people who had once lived there. That was important to me as well. She said that her teams always carried litter bags with them when they visited cemeteries and would make an effort to clean up the place a little before beginning their investigation. "Hopefully," Patti said of the spirits, "by showing respect for them, they'll work with us." Judging by the many videos and photos of spirit orbs and other anomalies she showed us, her system worked.

All that day, Patti went on in rapid-fire fashion, overwhelming us poor students with her knowledge. This lady knew her stuff: vortices, ectomist, intelligent hauntings, poltergeists, orbs, crisis hauntings, sleep paralysis (also called "old hag's syndrome"), portals, dowsing, electronic voice phenomena (EVP), electromagnetic frequency (EMF) meters, solar weather. These were just some of the things we learned about.

Most of the time my fellow students sat in stunned silence—I'm certain they were awake—and asked few questions. I was filling up a journal with notes. After a few hours we took a lunch break. Chuck joined us, wearing his own Ghost Chasers vest and an Indiana Jones hat. We drove to nearby Ryan's restaurant, where Patti and Chuck were well known to the staff because they always brought their students there.

After lunch, Patti continued her lecture, but we all got the opportunity to play around with some of the various pieces of electronic ghosthunting equipment Patti unpacked from foam-lined plastic cases. TriField meter, Multidetektor meter, CellSensor meter, Gaussmeter, E.L.F. meter, Infrared thermometer—you name it, Patti had it. We passed the instruments around and tried them out in the conference room, to a cacophony of chirping, buzzing, and beeping that sounded as if it were a rainforest full of drunken insects. After a few minutes of that, Patti collected the equipment, summarized some of her main points, and concluded the class, referring us to the Certificate of Completion enclosed in our purple folders.

So, I had passed Ghosthunting 101, but I was still not certified. The next step was Advanced Ghost Hunting, which would meet on a Saturday two weeks later. That class promised to be exciting, because a major portion of it involved an actual investigation of a haunted location. Only a few days before the advanced class was to meet, Patti called me to say that no one else had registered for that particular Saturday. She explained to me that, because she offers classes so often, students could pick and choose when they wanted to attend. Ever the professional, however, Patti offered to hold the class, even if I was the only student.

That Saturday I arrived in Lexington in the middle of a snowstorm, big wet flakes the size of half-dollars swirling down from the leaden sky. As I expected, I was the only student.

Patti and Chuck pulled into the parking lot just as I was getting out of my car and I helped carry some of their equipment inside. Once again, Patti set up in the conference room, and she insisted that she conduct the course as if there were more than a single student present.

It would be valuable practice for her, she said. How could I object to being privately tutored?

She handed me two spiral-bound manuals she had written that contained information for this part of the course, as well as the previous introductory lesson. Again using PowerPoint and her videos, Patti was off and running.

The snow was still coming down by the time we broke for lunch, but now it had changed into tiny pellets, and there was no significant accumulation. I sat in the backseat of Patti's Buick, behind Chuck, while she drove the three of us to Ryan's. The restaurant, known for its pig-out buffet, was crowded with Kentucky National Guardsmen, and the three of us drew dubious looks from them, probably because Patti and Chuck were wearing their own Ghost Chasers uniforms. We packed on several hundred calories, preparatory to our investigation later—you never know when you might eat again during a ghosthunt—then headed back to the office.

Because of the inclement weather Patti decided not to do an investigation at the Witches' Cemetery in Lexington, as she would typically do. Instead, she said we could do one right there, in the building. She and Chuck, as well as some of her students, had experienced paranormal activity in the sprawling structure.

"I won't tell you any more than that," Patti said, so as not to prejudice my findings in any way. "We'll just see what we get."

"Okay by me," I said.

We assembled our gear in the conference room. I had brought my own dowsing rods (never leave home without them) and stuck them through my belt. I tucked my digital camera into my shirt pocket and carried a small tape recorder, pen, and notepad. Now I understood Patti's Ghost Chasers vest, which she was loading with meters, thermometer, camera, and tape recorder, leaving her hands free to dowse.

I should explain that, though I've seen other ghosthunters use dowsing rods, I've never seen anyone use them in quite the same way as Patti. Her rods were twice as long as mine, heavier and thicker, and made of brass, whereas mine were chrome. She has "trained" her rods to answer her questions; when the rods cross, that is a "yes" answer, and when they move apart from each other, that is a "no" answer. She begins by asking three questions: May I dowse? Can I dowse? Should I dowse? She explains that the first question is simply asking permission of the spirits to dowse. The second is asking whether or not the dowser has the ability at that particular time to dowse successfully. The third question asks whether or not there is some unknown reason why the dowser should not dowse at that time. Patti will not dowse if she gets a "no" answer to any of these questions.

Assuming the spirits have given her the green light, she will walk through the location, literally following the direction of the rods. When she reaches an area in which the rods cross, she tests for the presence of a ghost. Using only one rod, she will ask a series of questions about gender, age, circumstances of death, and so forth, to help identify the spirit. She considers the answer to be "yes" when the rod bobs up and down and "no" when it wags from side to side. Once she has found this ghostly hot spot and asked some questions, she will also take pictures, run the tape recorder, and perform other measurements to try and corroborate the findings of the dowsing rods.

So, all packed and ready to go, we first held hands as Patti recited an opening prayer in which she asked for a blessing on our investigation and protection from any negative influences.

We set off through Chuck's extensive art gallery, a labyrinth of narrow corridors, small alcoves, and rooms, nearly every inch of vertical space hung with equestrian art, and at the rear, storage and work areas. The gallery was closed for the day and Chuck had left the building for a while, so Patti and I wandered the dimly lit halls alone. Patti was using an EMF meter, but wasn't getting any unusual readings until she stepped into the ladies' room. There the meter went crazy, a series of short clicks building up into a continuous loud buzz.

"Wow! What's that about?" I said.

"I don't know," Patti said. "Here, why don't you try it and see if you get the same thing." She handed me the meter.

We traded places and I stepped into the little room. I held the meter, moved it around, and, sure enough, started picking up something. The meter was whining loudly when I turned and faced a set of folding doors.

"Let's see what's behind here," I said, pulling open one of the doors.

There it was. My ghost was an electrical circuit box.

Patti said she didn't know the box was there, but I was suspicious. This was the ladies' room in her husband's building and she conducted classes in the building all the time. How could she not have known the box was there? On the other hand, it was a great way to teach a student how to determine a false reading from a genuine one. Sly, I thought, but effective.

We continued walking through the building, taking pictures and paying attention to the dowsing rods. In a work area at the rear of the building, my dowsing rods swung inward and crossed over each other. I stopped in my tracks.

"Whoa, got something," I said. I took a few steps forward and the rods swung open. When I walked back to my original position, they crossed once more.

"Stay there," Patti said. "Let me take some pictures." She moved about 10 feet away and began taking pictures using her digital camera. "Ask some questions," she said. "Ask if it's male or female."

I returned the rods to a neutral position and asked aloud if the spirit was a woman. They didn't move. "Are you a man?" I asked and they crossed, indicating "yes."

"Oh, wow!" Patti said. "I took a picture when you asked that and got an orb right by your rods."

"Really?"

I asked a few more questions and discovered that the spirit was an elderly black man who had died on that spot about 50 years ago.

"Let's try something," Patti said. She told me to put my camera down and to hold out my hand. "I do this all the time with spirits, to prove that we are actually talking to them and that they understand," she said to me. "Sweet spirit," Patti said, "if you can hear me and understand me, would you please go to John's hand? We don't mean you any harm. We are simply interested in you and would like to make contact with you."

I kept my hand held out. Patti took a picture.

"Nothing that time," she said. "Sweet spirit," she repeated, "I know it may be hard for you to do as we request, but we would appreciate it if you could try. Please, if you can, go to John's hand."

Patti took a few more pictures.

"There's an orb right by your elbow, John," Patti said excitedly, "and another on the other side of you. This is great. Thank you, sweet spirit!" she said.

We switched places and I took pictures of Patti using her digital camera because, as she said, it already had her energy on it. She stood with her left hand raised as I had done and once again she called to the "sweet spirit" to come to her hand. I looked through the viewfinder, saw nothing but Patti with her upturned hand, and took her picture. When we looked back at the picture, there was a white ball of light floating just above her hand.

Damn! This was pretty impressive stuff. Sure, I'd taken pictures before and captured orbs—many of which turned out to be dust, pollen,

A spirit drops by to speak with the author during
Patti Starr's ghosthunting class.
Courtesy of John Kachuba.

or water droplets—but this was an entirely different phenomenon. Patti would direct the spirit to a particular location and take a photo—and there it was, just where she had asked it to be. I could not account for it.

At that moment Chuck returned.

"How's it going?" he asked.

"Great," Patti said. "We got some orb pictures and John detected a spirit with his dowsing rods."

"Oh?" Chuck said, turning to me.

"Yes, the spirit of an elderly black man," Patti said.

Chuck nodded his head but was not at all surprised. "Did you tell him?" he asked his wife.

"No, let's wait a little," Patti said. "After the EVPs."

"Fine," Chuck said.

What was going on here, I wondered. What weren't they telling me? Why not? I suddenly realized I didn't know these folks all that well and I was in a big, dark building with them. But we had said a prayer before we started, hadn't we? Just the way the missionary had said grace with the cannibals.

"In fact, I think we're ready to do those EVPs now," Patti said. "Let's get some chairs."

We grouped three chairs together and seated ourselves. We were going to see if we could record spirit voices. I turned my tape recorder on and set it on a small table nearby. Patti attached her tape recorder to an amplifier so that when she played it back we would be able to hear better any sounds that may have been recorded. We turned off all the lights.

Patti explained that she would ask a question of the spirits, and after she asked it we were to sit perfectly still and absolutely quiet for one minute. Then she would play back that segment to discover if the tape recorder had, in fact, picked up any sound we did not actually hear at the time. In the meantime, my recorder would run continually as a backup. As with the photos, she politely addressed the "sweet spirit" and asked it to make itself known to us on the tape. We waited each time in the darkness, the only sounds being a sudden gust of wind outside or the occasional post-prandial stomach gurgling courtesy of Ryan's. But those sounds we recognized.

After several tries that yielded no results, Chuck suggested to Patti that maybe he should talk to the spirits and see if they would respond to him. Patti agreed.

"Now, Henry," Chuck said, in a loud voice, as I wondered who Henry was, "I know you're here. I heard you back here earlier this morning."

What? When?

"We don't mean to scare you or harm you in any way," Chuck said. "We just want to talk with you. If you could speak to us, or if you can't do that, if you could make some sound, some noise, to prove to us that you are here, we would be grateful for that."

We waited. Nothing. Chuck tried a few more times, but the spirit cat had apparently gotten the spirit's tongue. We turned on the lights.

"Okay," I said. "Who is this Henry?"

"He's our ghost," Patti said. Chuck got up and left the room. "According to a psychic who investigated the building, he was an elderly black man, just as you discovered, who died here about 50 years ago."

"In this building?"

"No," Chuck said from the doorway. He was holding a large photo in his hand. "This was open land 50 years ago, but there was something on this site. Look at this." He handed me the photo. It was an aerial view that showed a large white circus or carnival tent set in a patch of otherwise undeveloped property. "That's a photo of this property. We don't know for sure what the tent was about, but the psychic that came here saw a mental image of tigers, so we think it might have been a circus."

"And Henry? How does he fit into this?" I asked.

"He had something to do with the animals. Maybe a trainer or handler, we really don't know. Anyway, he died on this spot."

"Other students and investigators got the same impressions you did, John," Patti said, "so there's something going on here."

I nodded. Something did seem to be going on there for sure. I could not explain away the orbs that seemed to follow our commands. They defied logic and reason. But, as Patti had said earlier, ghosthunting was not a science, so maybe a ghosthunter had to suspend any notions of logic or reason in order to be open to new ideas. Certainly, no scientist would do that.

Back in the conference room, we said a closing prayer and then Patti presented me with my official Ghost Hunter Certification, earned under the auspices of Ghost Chasers International, Inc. I was now official. I couldn't wait to show my certificate to the next cop who pulled me over, or better yet, to the waitress at Pizza Hut.

Patti Star attracts a spirit in her ghosthunting class.
Courtesy of John Kachuba.

The author makes friends with a spirit at Patti Starr's ghosthunting class.
Courtesy of John Kachuba.

Chapter 9

The Spookiest Little Town in the Southwest

Las Vegas, New Mexico, may not have the glitz and glamour of its newer namesake in Nevada, but it does have something that won't be found in any casino: ghosts. With more than 900 buildings listed on the National Register of Historic Places, and a wild and wooly history revolving around the Santa Fe Trail, Hispanic pioneers, gunslingers, Indians, and even Rough Riders, it should come as no surprise that several ghosts call this northern New Mexico town home.

In the mid-1800s the Santa Fe Trail passed right through the town's plaza, bringing with it thousands of people seeking opportunity in the West. The town thrived as a provisioning center for these travelers. In 1879, the arrival of the Atchison, Topeka and Santa Fe Railroad made the trail obsolete but turned Las Vegas into the major commercial center of the southwest. People kept coming to Las Vegas, although many of these newcomers were not necessarily model citizens. Saloons flourished, and disputes were often settled in a hail of bullets. In those notorious times the streets of Las Vegas saw the likes of Wyatt Earp, Billy the Kid, Jesse James, Bob Ford, Doc Holliday, Mysterious Dave Brown, and other colorfully named desperados such as Rattlesnake Sam, Cock-Eyed Frank, Web-Fingered Billy, and Stuttering Tom. Gangs of vigilantes and Hispanic bandits, such as Los Gorros Blancos (The White Caps) helped to make the town one of the most lawless and dangerous places in the southwest. Miguel Otero, New Mexico territorial governor from 1897 to 1906, said of the men of Las Vegas, "They are as tough a bunch of bad men as ever gathered outside a penal institution."

The Plaza Hotel, built in 1882, was a silent witness to much of the town's violence, including the public hangings performed from a windmill erected upon the plaza. The grisly hanging windmill is long gone and the formerly dusty plaza is now covered with grass and shaded by trees, but the Victorian-era Plaza Hotel looks the same as it did when it first opened, and still offers guests a comfortable place to hang their hats. In fact, the hotel is so comfortable that at least one long-time resident refuses to leave.

The Plaza Hotel in Las Vegas, New Mexico.
Courtesy of John Kachuba.

Byron T. Mills was an attorney who bought the hotel, then known as the Landmark Hotel, sometime around 1918. Although he lived in the hotel, Mills was not interested in keeping it operational. He sold off much of the original furniture and rented the building as a dormitory for students. Mills's plan was to demolish the three-story brick landmark. Perhaps he had a last-minute change of heart, or simply ran out of time, but Mills died before the hotel could be torn down.

Mills's ghost haunts the third floor of the hotel, and Byron T's, the hotel bar, was named in his honor. The ghost is partial to the ladies—more than one female guest has reported hearing footsteps in her room or feeling some invisible presence sit on her bed. I spoke with Judy Finley, the Plaza Hotel's catering and marketing manager, who told me about one clearly distraught woman who came down to the front desk in the wee hours of the morning.

"The woman said she couldn't get to sleep because the ghost was bothering her," Judy said, "walking around and sitting on her bed. She left the hotel in her pajamas and drove around town the rest of the night. She came back in the morning and checked out."

Wid Slick is the present owner of the Plaza Hotel and is responsible for its renovation and restoration. Tall and slim, with white hair and beard, and wearing a vest and jeans, Wid resembled the quintessential cowboy. We sat in the Landmark Grill, the hotel's restaurant, as we talked. Wid has never seen the ghost of Byron T. but he knows that people have had uncanny experiences in the hotel, especially the restaurant staff.

"There was a lot of tension in the kitchen," Wid said. "The workers were acting crazy; they were being very unfriendly to each other. We brought in this Native American woman who detected what she said were bad spirits there and she did some rituals to get rid of them. There's been no trouble in the kitchen since then."

"So, Byron T. is gone?" I asked.

"Oh, no," said Wid. "What was going on in the kitchen had nothing to do with Byron T. People continue to smell his cigar smoke, hear footsteps, and things like that on the third floor."

Another haunted Las Vegas hotel is the El Fidel. The hotel was built in 1923 as the Meadows Hotel (las vegas is Spanish for "the meadows") and the hotel still boasts its original lobby. It was in this lobby that a tragic shooting took place in 1923.

Newspaper editor Carl Magee had written some damaging stories about Judge David Leahy, accusing the judge of corruption. Magee had been convicted on contempt charges but was pardoned by the New Mexico governor. Magee was in the El Fidel lobby when Judge Leahy walked in, and a dispute erupted. The judge went after Magee with his cane. The reporter pulled out a pistol and shot at the judge. His shot was wild and missed the judge, killing an innocent bystander instead. Acquitted of manslaughter charges, Magee moved to Oklahoma, where he achieved fame and fortune by inventing the parking meter.

Ghosts still linger in the El Fidel, however. The smoke from their ghostly stogies still wafts through the halls, and disembodied voices whisper in the air. Some guests have reported that Room 107 will often turn cold as death.

**

If ghosts need hotels for their comfort, might they not also need restaurants for their sustenance? How else can I explain the ghost at the El Norteno restaurant?

Jennifer and Ray Velasquez are the young owners of El Norteno. As I worked on an order of deep-fried avocado stuffed with chicken, the house specialty, Jennifer told me that she had always had the ability to sense other presences. But she was not alone in detecting ghosts in the restaurant, which occupies a building that was once a doctor's office.

"One of my waitresses was working during a storm," Jennifer said, "and the lights went out. When they came back on again, she saw a bald man in pajamas standing at the top of the stairs. Then he disappeared."

I looked over at the stairs, which where wide and open; a person standing there would be clearly seen by anyone on the ground floor.

"Pajamas?" I asked.

Jennifer shrugged. "That same bald man has been seen reflected in the bathroom mirror," she said.

She went on to say that a friend of hers who is also sensitive to spirits came to the restaurant for the first time and immediately felt the presence of an unseen male, a bald man "wearing a suit." She had not been told anything about the previous sightings of the ghost.

Jennifer also told me about the time a waitress was about to go upstairs to punch in on the time clock. The light switch for the upstairs room is at the head of the stairs. As she approached the stairs, the lights suddenly came on. There was no one upstairs who could have thrown the switch; the waitress decided to punch in later.

The El Norteno ghost must like playing with lights. One day, as Ray was working in the restaurant alone, he said aloud that he wished he had more light. Additional lights suddenly came on by themselves. Ray could find no explanation for them turning on.

* * *

Another favorite haunt of Las Vegas's spirits is the Adele Ilfeld Auditorium on the campus of New Mexico Highlands University. Charles Ilfeld was a prosperous merchant who helped fund the construction of the auditorium in 1914 in memory of his late wife, Adele. It is a beautiful sandstone building built in a Romanesque Revival style, with heavy Roman arches and slender Tuscan columns. As I ascended the staircase to the entrance, I felt as though I was entering some ancient basilica in Rome. Inside the cool and dimly lit lobby, Donna Martinez, the audi-

Ilfeld Auditorium at New Mexico Highlands University, in Las Vegas.
Courtesy of John Kachuba.

torium's manager for the last 13 years, met me. We walked down into the theatre, now hushed and still.

Donna told me that a drama professor from the university died in the theatre in 1978. He had been there alone and his body was discovered the next day lying in the wings on stage. Is his spirit still on stage? No one knows, but some people think that Adele Ilfeld's ghost can be found backstage.

"Sometimes, the set people in a stage production are unable to open the tool room door," Donna said. "No matter what they do, they can't get it open. They have to ask Adele nicely and then they can open the door.

"There are other ghosts here as well," Donna continued. "People have seen a man in a trench coat standing in the balcony." I looked up at the balcony. All I could see were empty rows of seats disappearing into the gloom at the back of the theatre. Was there something else in those murky shadows watching us?

Donna also told me that people had seen a ghostly clown on stage and that the theatre house manager had seen a little blond-haired boy upstairs in the office area as she was closing the theatre following a children's' performance. She caught only a glimpse of him, and when she went to look for the boy, she could not find him. There was no one else in the theatre at the time.

Donna Martinez has had her own ghostly encounter in the auditorium. She told me that, just as a quartet of musicians was finishing its performance, the house lights began to dim in synchronicity with the quartet's last notes. The audience might have thought that the fading light was part of the performance, but it was not.

"All the lights faded, and then the house went completely dark for a moment, before the lights came back on," Donna said. "It was a total blackout, which is impossible, since all the lights are on separate circuits. It wasn't a power failure, either, since we had other power."

Perhaps the light show was Adele Ilfeld's way of showing her approval for the quartet's performance.

* * *

There are other theatrical ghosts in Las Vegas. Just a few miles out of town the United World College, established by industrialist Armand

Hammer in 1982, sits perched on a pine-studded peak, its landmark sandstone turret piercing the cloudless New Mexico sky. Originally built as a hotel in 1882 to take advantage of the nearby hot springs, the building that is now the home of United World College is a massive sandstone structure surrounded by wide verandahs. Fully 200 students from all around the world study at the college to earn an international baccalaureate degree, and acclaimed scholars and artists often visit the college.

United World College in Las Vegas, New Mexico.
Courtesy of John Kachuba.

The college's ghost is that of an opera diva who was a guest at the then-hotel in the 1880s. She was practicing her music in the circular ground floor room of the turret when her husband, who accused her of adultery, confronted her—confronted her very sharply: He stabbed her to death.

My guide during my visit to United World College was a young man named Jeremiah, himself a graduate of the college. As we stood before the massive fireplace in the ornately paneled lobby of the college, Jeremiah told me that students through the years have heard opera arias echoing in the halls of the building late at night Apparently, even death cannot silence the diva.

* * *

Unearthly sounds are also heard at Fort Union National Monument, located in a windswept valley 20 miles north of Las Vegas. The wind whispers as it whips through the adobe ruins of the fort, originally built in 1851 to protect the Santa Fe Trail, and sighs through the prairie grasses and fields of wild sunflowers. But the wind cannot explain the eerie sounds some of the park rangers have heard emanating from a site at which the remains of several Indians were uncovered, the bones of each showing signs of violent death.

The ruins of Fort Union, New Mexico.
Courtesy of John Kachuba.

In addition to the role they played in defending the Santa Fe Trail from marauding bands of Indians, troops from Fort Union were also instrumental in the 1862 Civil War Battle of Glorieta Pass, in which a Confederate invasion of the New Mexico Territory was repulsed. That battle, though locally important, was not of the magnitude of typical Civil War battles fought east of the Mississippi River; there were a total of 331 casualties. One poor soldier from that battle has had a difficult time accepting his own death, according to park ranger Valerie Duran.

The sky over Fort Union the day I visited was so hard and blue I felt I could reach up and rap it with my knuckles. I noticed a solitary hawk circling overhead as I walked along the gravel paths of the fort, listening to Valerie's running commentary on the fort's history. As is my wont, I asked her about ghosts.

She told me that rangers at the fort often heard the sounds of horses, wagons, and people, but she cautioned me that the sounds could be simply carried on the wind from area ranches. I scanned the horizon in all directions and couldn't see any ranches nearby, but, okay, I was willing to give her that explanation, especially because she told me about the dead soldier.

"There was a ranger on duty at the visitors' center," Valerie said, "and it was getting to be time to close the park for the day. He saw a man outside the window and went out to tell him that the park would be closing soon." Valerie paused. I could barely see her eyes in the shade cast by her broad-brimmed Smokey the Bear hat. The wind whistled around the ruins of an adobe chimney. "When the ranger spoke to the man, he answered by saying that 'a lot had changed at the fort.' Then the ranger noted that the man's clothes were old and worn. The man then told the ranger that he had accidentally shot himself at Glorieta and that he had returned to Fort Union because he didn't know where else to go. Then he disappeared."

Valerie looked up and now I could see her eyes. They showed no guile; clearly she thought what so many people in the Las Vegas area also thought: In the Land of Enchantment, surely there must be ghosts.

CHAPTER 10

THE GHOST DETECTIVE

When Dr. Andrew Nichols was only 12 years old, a ghost visited him.

"My sister had been killed in an automobile accident," Nichols said, during my conversation with him in his Gainesville, Florida, office, "and for several months after her death I had been having a series of recurring dreams—nightmares—about her death. One night I awakened, or at least at the time I thought I was awake, and saw her standing in my room. She looked completely solid as most apparitions do. She didn't say anything, but was smiling at me, and when I got out of bed and took a step toward her, she suddenly disappeared."

Nichols is a parapsychologist and the founder and director of the American Institute of Parapsychology. A leading authority in the paranormal and the author of *The Ghost Detective*, Nichols has investigated more than 600 cases of paranormal activity in his 25-year career. Following is the conversation I had with Nichols.

What did that apparition mean to you?

There were two aspects of that experience which I have consistently found to be true throughout my investigations in the years subsequent to that experience. Number one was that the experience was transformative, and these experiences often are; they transform your life. Once you have an experience like that you are never quite the same again. I wouldn't be sitting

Dr. Andrew Nichols.
Courtesy of John Kachuba.

here now if it weren't for that experience. That's what got me interested in parapsychology. It changed the entire course of my life. The second aspect of it was that it was a very healing experience. Most people think of ghosts as being frightening occurrences, but in many cases they are actually healing and transformative. That experience was healing for me because I never again had another nightmare about my sister's death. I still dream about her from time to time but it is just childhood memories, that sort of thing. I have never had another nightmare about her death, so it healed me.

Now, whether or not you believe that that was actually my sister returned from the grave to comfort me, even though she didn't speak, the message was clear: I am okay, don't worry about me. Whether or not you believe that was actually her or whether you believe it was an artifact of my psyche that I generated because I needed to see it, I needed to be healed; either way it is an extraordinary experience.

Which leads me into the most important question: Are ghosts real?

That is just about the most open-ended question I can imagine. The question is, what do you believe is a ghost? How do you define a ghost? The simple answer is I believe that people genuinely experience ghosts. There is no question about it—people do experience apparitions, but whether or not they exist objectively is the key issue.

How can we prove that ghosts exist? Are the many ghosthunting groups on the right track?

[Nichols leaned back in his chair, one arm resting on the desk. He looked positively Freudian with his glasses, Vandyke beard, and moustache.] I pioneered some of what they're doing, not just me alone, but a couple of other investigators like Lloyd Auerbach, who have been around for many, many years. We were the first to use EMF meters in investigations, but now it has gotten ridiculous. Most of the groups really do not understand how to use their equipment. They don't really understand what it is they are measuring; they don't understand the limitations of the technology. If ghosts were objectively verifiable, well-funded scientists in the physics labs would have discovered them a long time ago. They would not be discovered by people with Radio Shack equipment. That's just the reality. I think these groups are chasing their tails personally, but I started out doing the same thing because I think it is certainly something we needed to find out. We needed to find out whether ghosts are objectively measurable or quantifiable and, although I don't think the question has been completely put to rest, I am now very skeptical of that component.

Personally, I believe that ghosts are a subjective experience. They are seen in the mind's eye. They appear to be out there in the three-dimensional space, but in fact, they are a type of hallucination. Although, I will qualify that by saying that in some cases they are a hallucination with an ESP component, which allows people to acquire information that they could not have acquired through their physical senses only. In other words, they might see an apparition of a person and then it turns out later that the person actually lived or died in that location and that they had no way of knowing that beforehand.

But if ghosts are hallucinations, how can we explain haunted houses and places where many people over the years witness the same phenomena?

Well, there are legitimate hauntings, although my definition of a haunting may differ from that of many people. I don't believe that a haunting is necessarily a place inhabited by spirits and ghosts, but rather a haunting or haunt is any location where people repeatedly experience the paranormal, or what they describe as paranormal. That includes visual apparitions, but also sounds suggestive of human activity: footsteps, voices, sensations of being watched, or sensations of a presence, sensations of fear, cold spots, unusual odors, tactile sensations, and so forth. Hallucinations can be visual, auditory, olfactory, or tactile. In fact, the only sense that doesn't seem to be affected is taste. I have never heard of anyone tasting a ghost, but all the other senses seem to be activated. So, there are places where the space seems to be modified in some way. Now, the mechanism by which this occurs is completely a mystery to us. We looked at a number of different possible mechanisms, including a type of electromagnetic imprint from emotionally charged states.

Everyone knows that a number of hauntings are associated with violence: murders, suicides, battles; so it seems that powerful emotional states would generate some type of electromagnetic distortion or imprint similar to a holographic projection. This would be sequestered within the physical structure of the building, or woods, or wherever. Suitably sensitive people could tap into it.

I did a 10-year study of electromagnetic and psychological aspects of hauntings. This was a study supported by a grant, and the conclusion was that there is an electromagnetic or geomagnetic component to these cases. But, I don't think what we are measuring is the ghost; what we are measuring are magnetic field anomalies created usually by a geological source, like underground water, or earthquake faults, or concentrations of iron ore. All these things can cause very localized distortions in the earth's electromagnetic field with abrupt field reversals in the Earth's polarity. What we find is that certainly people's brains are sensitive to these electromagnetic fields, and this may be the answer to the haunted house, because living in a place like that, these fields trigger these experiences in sensitive individuals. That is why people tend to have these experiences repeatedly in the same locations. My research supported that theory. There were unusual magnetic fields in approximately 80 percent of the cases that I felt were strong cases of haunting. So, there are two possibilities: Either these fields trigger genuine psychic experiences, or they trigger hallucinatory experiences that are purely psychological but that still appear paranormal. I think it is a combination of both.

Are there other theories, besides electromagnetism, that might explain haunted houses?

I believe that it has to do with the nature of time because these are really retrocognitive experiences, just as we have precognitive experiences, which are very well established as ESP. Even though there are many mainstream scientists that are still quite skeptical about ESP, telepathy, and precognition, all of them have been well established in rigorously controlled laboratory studies. As far as I am concerned, anyone who still insists that it is unproven is just ignorant of the facts. Usually, when people experience the past it is when they are in an altered state of consciousness. Most ghostly experiences occur while the individual is in an altered state of consciousness. This is why ghosthunters so infrequently experience ghosts, because they conduct vigils, and the problem with vigils is you must be vigilant. Vigilance is counterproductive to seeing ghosts. I am convinced of that.

Do you mean to say that we dream ghosts?

About 80 percent of all paranormal events occur in dream states, the cognitive dreams, telepathic dreams, out-of-body experiences, and so on. Also, reported contacts with the dead. So, the dream seems to be the number-one paranormal-inducing state, closely followed by hypnogogic types of states, on the edge of sleep, which are dream-like themselves, but not quite the same thing.

Whenever someone tells me they've seen a ghost, I ask, what were you doing when you saw the ghost? If they say, "I was just falling asleep," or "Something woke me up and there it was," similar to the experience I had with my sister, then there is little question in my mind that it was a type of hypnogogic hallucination.

So, ghosts are merely hallucinations?

The vast majority of apparitional experiences occur in those states. I think the reason there aren't more reported is that when people have REM dreams involving the dead, or anytime we dream of a person, whether they are alive or dead, that is basically an apparitional experience. We don't describe it as such because we think of it as just a dream. So, we might, if it has some seeming correlation with an external event that we could not have inferred, tend to think of it as a paranormal dream. But when we have these hypnogogic, hypotonic experiences, then we think we are awake. People will swear up and down that they were awake, and they truly believe that they were, because part of the brain is asleep and part of the brain is awake and we really can't distinguish between those states.

In other words, ghosts are all in our head. Is that right?

I have to be very careful in how I explain this because when I try to explain it people say, well you are saying that it is all in my head, or you are saying it was just a dream, but I think we are proceeding from false assumptions. The problem is assuming that dreams are just dreams. I think dreams are much more than just dreams. I think dreams themselves are highly significant and highly underrated, but on top of that, they are the most conducive to genuine ESP experiences.

[Nichols went on to explain that ESP signals come to us in the form of visual images, rather than thoughts, and that, if we receive these images during states of altered consciousness (dreaming, near-sleep, meditation), they can appear to us as being real, "out there."]

There is also reverie, which is when people are engaged in some repetitive task, usually one that they have done many times, like washing dishes or vacuuming the rug. Their minds are just open and wandering. You can be wide-awake in those reverie states, but still your mind is drifting and very open. That is another time that people commonly see ghosts. They would then describe it as a ghost because they would say, I was wide-awake, I was vacuuming the rugs. Obviously there is no question that I wasn't asleep. But, in fact, people's minds do drift into states resembling sleep. It is called micro-sleep. Truck drivers do it all the time when they are on long haul. They might fall asleep six times during the hour and never even know that they were asleep because it was so momentary. Most apparitional experiences are very momentary. So, I think that these are basically hallucinatory experiences. But a certain percentage of them have a psi [psychic] or ESP component to them, so they may accurately reflect what went on in the past and the history of a certain location, or they may reflect what is going on in a distant location with a living person. As you know, many people see apparitions of the living, not just the dead, as well as animals and inanimate objects, and all sorts of things, which is a big argument against it being a soul-type situation.

A good example of an apparitional experience that did not involve a deceased person was the woman who sent her 11-year-old daughter down to the convenience store to get some milk. This was in the afternoon. The woman then turned and was washing the dishes and was undoubtedly in one of those reverie states. She got the feeling that someone was watching her. She turned around and there was her daughter standing in the kitchen. She had kind of a sad look on her face, she didn't have anything in her hands, but her dress was wet. The mother said to her, "What happened? Did you drop the milk?" At that point the daughter just disappeared. The mother immediately got a feeling that something was terribly wrong and went running out of the house down the street and as she approached the convenience store she saw the lights of the police cars and the ambulance. It turned out the little girl had been hit by a car coming out of the store and had dropped the milk. It had splashed all over her dress in the way the mother had seen it. The little girl wasn't dead, but she was seriously injured. So, it wasn't her soul her mother saw, unless her soul can be in two places at once, but rather, it seemed to be a telepathic communication between mother and daughter which manifested itself in the form of a visual hallucination because she happened to be in that reverie at the time she received that impulse, that telepathic impulse. Does that make sense?

Yes, I understand.

Let me emphasize that I do not believe that the majority of apparitional experiences have any extrasensory component. The vast majority of them are just purely subjective. But there are some startling cases, like the one I just described to you, where there does seem to be a real extrasensory component.

Okay, I've got that, but I'm still not certain how it is people actually see ghosts.

First of all it is important to realize that all perception takes place in the brain, but you have two sources of data, which can be processed by perception into imagery. One source of data is external, reflective light entering through our eyes. That is organized into models in the brain from which we get imagery. I see that lamp over there, which is really just a model in my brain of that lamp. The second source of imagery is internal, as in dreams, where we have an internal source of stimulation, which the brain then organizes into visual imagery, such as when we have a dream at night. Even though we have our eyes closed, we are still experiencing imagery. So, what is happening with a ghost is that you have your eyes open so you have an external source of stimulation, but you also simultaneously have an internal source of imagery, which is superimposed over the external source. Now this creates a struggle because, not only does the brain have to create the image of the apparition, but it also has to selectively negate the incoming data. In other words, for me to see an apparition as solid, not only does the image have to be created, but my brain also has to selectively deactivate the information that is trying to come through where that apparition is seen.

Is that because the brain is just trying to identify or make sense of the apparition? File it in the proper mental drawer?

It is more than that. It is really remarkable. If I saw an apparition standing between this lamp and me, the information from that lamp is still entering my eye. So, in order for the apparition to appear solid, the brain has to selectively deactivate only that information and not the information coming from the rest of the room. It allows that in, but only the information that is blocked by the inner apparition has to be negated so that it is not perceived, which is remarkable when you think about it. You have overlay, but it is a struggle because that information is hard for the mind or the brain to keep from being perceived. So what happens, because most apparitions are usually no more than four or five seconds in duration, is as the brain looses its struggle, as it ceases to be able to generate that image to the extent that it can block out incoming data, then the image starts to become transparent. The data is leaking through, and as the external data wins, then the apparition is gone. It is just a theory, but it seems to make sense.

In the quiet of Dr. Nichols's office, our discussion continued on, covering a wide range of paranormal topics, far too many to include in this one chapter. As the conversation drew to a close, I asked Dr. Nichols if he had any final words.

We all have a powerful need to believe in life after death. We all have a destiny interest in the outcome of this particular question. It is impossible for us to study this and be unbiased. There is no question that I am biased. But the result of my bias has been that I tend to err more on the side of skepticism because of my bias, because I know I really do want this to be true like everyone else. I would like to be reunited with my sister. That is what drove me into this in the first place. But, because I know I am biased, the evidence that would be necessary to convince me of an afterlife would have to be so overwhelmingly strong that it would overcome any possible bias I would have. So far I haven't found that evidence.

At least, he hasn't found it yet.

CHAPTER 11

REAL GHOST WRITERS

Artists, whether they are painters, musicians, or writers, frequently attribute their inspiration to their muses. Others say that artists have just a touch of madness about them, an eccentric genius that helps them to create great works of art. However the impetus behind artistic expression is defined, it is often linked to some force outside the artist, something ethereal, perhaps divine, supernatural. It should be no surprise then that some of the greatest writers ever known continue to inhabit our earthly realm as true ghost writers.

Edith Wharton was a writer with a list of "firsts" attached to her name: the first woman to be awarded the Pulitzer Prize for Fiction (in 1921 for *The Age of Innocence*), the first woman to receive an honorary doctorate from Yale University, and the first woman to be elevated to full membership in the American Academy of Arts and Letters. Born in 1862 into fashionable Old New York society, Edith was not expected to do much with her life other than marry well, which she apparently did when she married Edward ("Teddy") Wharton in 1885. But the marriage was loveless and Edith suffered bouts of severe depression, relieved through her writing. At The Mount, the sprawling "cottage" the Whartons built in 1902 in the Berkshire Mountains of Massachusetts, Edith wrote nine books, including *Ethan Frome* and *The House of Mirth*. The latter book was immensely popular and gave her the courage to pursue her dream of writing; she wrote more than 40 books in 40 years. In 1911, her marriage in tatters, Edith moved to France, divorcing Teddy two years later. In

The Mount, Edith Wharton's home in the Berkshires.
Courtesy of John Kachuba.

her absence and without her permission, Teddy sold The Mount. Edith never saw it again, but said of it, "The Mount was my first real home, and its blessed influence still lives in me."

Yes, and she still lives in it.

It was a beautiful, sunny day in early August when my wife, Mary, and I visited The Mount. It had been hot as we drove north from Connecticut, but we left some of that uncomfortable heat behind as we climbed up into the leafy Berkshires' coolness. Every time I've driven through the little colonial towns of the Berkshires I've always been struck by two things—history and affluence—and, arriving at The Mount in Lenox, Massachusetts, brought those two things together. Even as we turned into the large gravel parking lot, the house itself was still some distance off, hidden somewhere in the shimmering New England woods.

There was a little kiosk at the edge of the parking lot where we bought admission tickets to the house. Because it was a weekday afternoon, there were very few visitors, so I had no qualms about chatting with the woman behind the window about ghosts. I thought that she would probably politely dismiss my inquiries—this was, after all, the tony estate of a celebrated and well-to-do author, not a carnival spook house—but I was wrong. She was as interested in ghost stories as me.

"Many of the guides think the place is creepy," she said, leaning closer to the window. "Me too."

"Why?" I asked.

"Well, it was my job to lock up the stable at night," she said, pointing to the big horse barn that stood just a few yards behind the kiosk and now housed an exhibit about The Mount. "One night when I was in there I heard footsteps walking across the floor above me. I thought I had been alone, so I called out to see if anyone was there. No one answered, so I got out of there and locked the doors. As for the house," she continued, "I won't go down there at night alone."

It wasn't night and I had Mary to protect me, so we walked down the leafy lane until we reached the "cottage." This was no cottage. The three-story white painted house, designed by Ogden Codman, working very closely with Edith Wharton (the two had coauthored *The Decoration of Houses* in 1897), is modeled upon Belton House, a 17th-century English country estate, and sprawls on a hill overlooking acres of formal gardens and orchards laid out in Italian villa style. The next guided tour of the house wasn't for half an hour, so we walked around back to the enormous stone terrace overlooking the gardens. There was a café set up there, and we sat at one of the wrought iron tables nibbling on sandwiches while waiting for the tour.

"Ah, it's good to be queen," Mary said, completely putting herself in the role of Edith Wharton, and I tried to calculate how many copies of my books I would have to sell to buy such a "cottage" for her.

While we waited I asked the two servers if they had heard of any ghost stories about the house, but they both replied that they had just started working there and didn't know much about the place.

When it was time, we went around to the front of the house, passed through a large wrought iron gate into a circular courtyard, and joined a group of a dozen or so people for the next tour. Our tour guide, a young man named Bryan led us inside. Many of the rooms on the main floor had been furnished and decorated by various influential interior designers to give a sense of how they could have looked in Edith's time. Edith's library was on that floor, although most of her collection of 2,000 books was no longer on the built-in shelves. Bryan told us that, despite the many photos that showed her seated at the desk in the library, Edith rarely wrote there, preferring instead to write from her bed in the early morning hours.

This was all very interesting, but not particularly ghostly.

Then we went up to the third floor, where Edith's bedroom was located, as was the guest bedroom used by writer Henry James, a close friend of both Edith and Teddy. Henry had visited at The Mount several times. The third floor had not yet been restored, and it showed much of the wear and tear the house had suffered after the Whartons moved out and before Edith Wharton Restoration eventually acquired it in 1980. An exhibit titled "Lily's Downfall" was set up on the third floor and featured six scenes from the life of Lily Bart, the heroine in *The House of Mirth*, each of them arranged in a separate room. Memorable lines from the novel were painted on the walls, and each room's tableau featured vintage clothing and accessories arranged on mannequins. The last scene was displayed in the large bedroom that had been used by Henry James, empty now except for the tableau, a simple bed in which lay the ghostly white figure of poor Lily, dead from an accidental overdose of chloral hydrate. The windows of the room had been fitted over with black coverings, so the room was dim, lit only by the small lamp on the bedside table. I stood there with the rest of the group, but when they passed out of the room, heading for the stairs, I remained behind.

What was I waiting for? I didn't know for sure, but I had read somewhere that the ghost of Henry James continued to visit the ghost of Edith Wharton at The Mount. What better place to get a sense of James than in the bedroom he occupied? But even in that dim room, in the silence, with the eerie figure of the dead woman in the bed, I did not feel him.

I caught up with the others as the tour concluded downstairs. I took Bryan aside and asked him what he knew about the ghosts at The Mount. He told me that most of the ghost stories seemed to originate from the days when a Shakespearean acting company lived in the house and presented plays there. There were about 20 members of the Shakespeare & Co. troupe, Bryan said, who, during their tenure in the house, experienced strange sounds and objects being moved or vanishing and reappearing later in a different location. Bryan was skeptical about the reports, however, chalking them up to actors being emotional and high-strung. That could be, I supposed, but some would say that it was exactly that type of psychological profile that would make them more sensitive to spirits; it's no accident that theatres everywhere always have a ghost light burning on the stage at night.

Although the formal tour was over, Mary and I lingered at The Mount. In the courtyard I chatted with Shelly, a guide who would be conducting the next tour, and asked her what she knew of the ghosts. Although she had never seen them herself, she told me that people had seen ghosts at the house.

"What did they look like?" I asked.

"One of them appears as a bearded man wearing a top hat," she said, and I recalled that Henry James had sported a beard for at least part of his life and had been photographed wearing a top hat. "The other is a woman who seems to be calling her dogs," Shelly said.

Edith Wharton loved dogs and always had them around, at least while she lived at The Mount. I had already seen the little pet cemetery in the woods near the house with several gravestones marking the final resting places of "Our Sweetheart Modele," "Our Friend Jules," "Mimi," "Toto" (so that's what became of Dorothy's dog), and several other furry friends. It would make sense that the ghost of Edith Wharton would still have her beloved pets with her.

"You know that Wharton was afraid of ghosts, don't you?" Shelly asked. No, I didn't know. "For many years she couldn't sleep in the same room with a ghost story, even one she had written herself."

"She wrote ghost stories?" I asked, clearly demonstrating how much I had forgotten over the years about American literature.

A pet's grave marker at The Mount.
Courtesy of John Kachuba.

I hurried back into the gift shop located in the house and, sure enough, there was a copy of The Ghost Stories of Edith Wharton, which I immediately purchased. It turned out that Edith had included an interesting "Autobiographical Postscript" in the collection that shed more light on her beliefs about ghosts. In the postscript Edith wrote that she contracted typhoid fever at the age of 9 while her family was visiting Mildbad in Germany's Black Forest. The local German doctor had never treated typhoid and told Edith's parents that their daughter was dying. Her parents refused to accept that grim prognosis and, upon hearing that the Russian Czar's personal physician was traveling through Mildbad, appealed to him for assistance. He visited Edith and changed the German doctor's "treatments," and the girl survived. During her convalescence, she read many books, one of them being what she called a "Celtic" book about ghosts, robbers, and the supernatural. That book affected her strongly.

Edith wrote in The Ghost Stories of Edith Wharton (Scribner, 1973) that she had formerly been a fearless child, but that she now lived in constant fear—of what, she did not know. Some dark, menacing presence seemed to follow her everywhere, lurking and threatening. She was conscious of it throughout the day, and she could only sleep if a nursemaid was in the room and the lights were left on. The young girl was especially aware of the formidable presence as she returned from her daily walks, which she always took with a maid or governess, or her father:

> ...While I waited on the door-step for the door to be opened, I could feel it behind me, upon me; and if there was any delay in the opening of the door I was seized by a choking agony of terror. It did not matter who was with me, for no one could protect me; but, oh, the rapture of relief if any companion had a latchkey, and we could get in at once, before it caught me!

> This species of hallucination lasted seven or eight years... before my heart ceased to beat with fear if I had to stand for half a minute on a door-step! I am often inclined—like most people—to think my parents might have brought me up in a manner more suited to my tastes and disposition; but I owe them the deepest gratitude for their treatment of me during this difficult phase. They made as light of my fears as they could, without hurting my feelings; but they never scolded or ridiculed me for them, or tried to "harden" me by making me sleep in the dark, or doing any of the things which are supposed to give courage to timid children. I believe it is owing to his kindness and forbearance that my terror gradually wore off, and that I became what I am now—a woman hardly conscious of physical fear. But how long the traces of my illness lasted may be judged from the fact that, till I was twenty-seven or twenty-eight, I could not sleep in the room with a book containing a ghost story, and that I have frequently had to burn books of this kind, because it frightened me to know that they were downstairs in the library!

Now, there was a writer who truly recognized the power of words.

It is interesting to note that Edith developed this sense of being haunted by something after a serious illness that nearly took her life. The paranormal literature is full of stories about people who develop psychic abilities after near-death experiences, and one has to wonder whether Edith's experiences were "hallucinations," as she writes, or whether they were actual psychic contacts with the paranormal world. Her fears persisted, in various forms, for 18 years; that's a lot of years to be suffering hallucinations. Could it be that Edith's fear was not so much fear of the hallucinations themselves, but perhaps a subconscious fear that she had contacted the psychic side of her personality, a contact she would not consciously have wanted to make? Perhaps it took her 18 years to deny and repress her natural psychic abilities.

This is mere speculation, of course, but it is important to note that many writers—and other artists—believed in and experienced psychic encounters that could only be termed ghostly, and some of them, such as Edith and Henry, may still be among us. The shade of Nathaniel Hawthorne is said to inhabit Salem, Massachusetts' House of the Seven Gables, while Edgar Allan Poe wanders his old home in Baltimore. Ernest Hemingway's ghost still types away on his battered typewriter in his Key West home, and F. Scott Fitzgerald may be rooming at Asheville, North Carolina's Grove Park Inn. And who was the ghost that haunted James Thurber's house in Columbus, Ohio, which he later wrote about in his short story "The Night the Ghost Got In"?

Mysteries, all, but maybe yet another writer should have the final word here. William Shakespeare's Hamlet spoke to his friend:

There are more things in heaven and earth,
Horatio, than are dreamt of in your philosophy.

CHAPTER 12
CAVEAT EMPTOR, CASPER

I saw two items posted recently on eBay that I would have loved to have bought, if I could have afforded them: haunted houses.

The first was a three-bedroom, three-bathroom house in Yankton, South Dakota, built in 1892. It sat on an acre of property only one block from Yankton's historic downtown. The house had a long haunted history and had been featured on CNN Headline News, the CBS radio network, and radio and television stations from New York, California, and Florida, and had been written about in USA Today, the Associated Press, and other news publications. Former owners of the house and renters had reported seeing a little boy wearing a flannel shirt who suddenly vanished; black orbs floating in the rooms; ghostly figures that appeared beside the beds of residents; cold spots; a picture that hung in the sitting room continually relocating itself to the floor in the middle of the room; and an electric fan that threw itself from one room to another.

The opening bid for the house was $85,100.

I contacted the owner of the house, Colleen Meyers, to see how the auction was going. The bidding was not as brisk as she would have liked, but there was interest in the house, even from people living abroad. Colleen said that she was selling the house partly because of the ghosts, but also because she and her son were animal lovers and needed more space for their growing menagerie.

Embedded with the Paranormal Paramilitary
Riding with Mediums, Spirit Seekers, and Ghost Hunters
130

But she doesn't downplay the ghostly activity in the house. "I do not feel the ghosts living here have been evil, mean, or bad in any way," she said. "When the fan flew across the room I felt it was a ghost or spirit warning me that my son was in danger. The times I woke up from sleepwalking at the top of the basement stairs, I felt I was woken up by a ghost who was trying to stop me from taking that last step toward falling down the stairs."

I spoke with Colleen again several months after the auction to find out what had happened. She told me she had been unable to sell the house, despite much interest in it. She had decided to turn it into a bed and breakfast establishment (or, as she called it, "Bed & Boo"). I wished her luck.

The second haunted house listed on eBay was in Atchison, Kansas, and had an opening bid of $500,000, or a "buy it now" price of $2,000,000. In Atchison, Kansas? I don't think so.

The house was billed as the home of Sallie the Heartland Ghost and was, according to its owners, haunted by two ghosts, a young girl they called Sallie and a woman in her 30s. A doctor who maintained his office in it formerly owned the house, and some people think that Sallie could have been a patient who died in the office from some illness. At the time the house was listed on eBay, it was vacant, the family having moved out because of the ghosts. The ghost woman supposedly attacked the husband on several occasions, leaving him with raw scratches on his body. He was nearly shoved over a stair railing by an unseen force.

Yep, it sounded like it was time to load the wagon.

As I read about these houses I wondered who would deliberately buy a haunted house, and why? I also wondered how you would know if a house you bought was haunted or not. Would the seller tell you? Would you even think to ask? Do the drapes stay? The refrigerator? What about the headless ghost?

I checked into this with some friends of mine, Judy and Bruce Leever. The Leevers live in Loveland, Ohio, and over the years had bought many houses, which they then resold or rented. To the best of their knowledge, they said, they had never purchased a haunted house, although they pointed out that Ohio real estate laws did not require such disclosure in the contract, so a buyer would never know. In Ohio, it was a case of caveat emptor (let the buyer beware).

Judy said that she would tell potential renters about a house that was supposed to be haunted, although she said she would probably make a joke about it. Bruce was of a different opinion.

"To hell with them," he said. "I wouldn't say a thing. It's their own fault if they believe in that [expletive deleted]."

"I think it would be interesting to own a haunted house," Judy added. "We did attempt to buy a house here in Loveland where there had been a recent murder. We didn't get it and someone else did buy it without any apparent problems."

I wondered if the principle of caveat emptor was common, as real estate laws differ from state to state. My cousin Ralph Durante lives near Jupiter, on Florida's Atlantic coast, where he sells real estate. He said that, as in Ohio, the state of Florida did not require a seller to reveal that a house was haunted.

"There is no verbiage like that in Florida contracts," Ralph said, "but if you want to stretch the point, there is a 'seller's disclosure' form in which the seller must disclose any facts known to the seller that may materially affect the value of the property that are not readily observable by the buyer or that have not been disclosed to the buyer."

Hmmm. I would think a ghost would qualify as a "not readily observable fact."

Ralph went on to say that Florida real estate contracts also included a phrase that the "seller extends and intends no warranty and makes no representation of any type, either expressed or implied, as to the physical condition or history of the property."

"Now what these things mean is open to interpretation," Ralph said. "As an example, Florida recently allowed the seller not to disclose that a murder was committed in the house."

My ears pricked up. "Murder? Then maybe there is a ghost as well. What do you think?" I asked.

"If a ghost exists I would think it would materially affect the value of the property," Ralph said, "but how does a buyer take me to court and prove that I knew about ghosts? If I believe they do not exist, then everything that I hear related to them I would just discredit, and I have no obligation to tell the seller or buyer about rumors."

Most states' real estate laws do not specifically address the forms the deceased may take in the afterlife, but they do address the stigma attached to a house in which a death may have occurred. There are varying degrees to which a house may be "stigmatized," of course. A single death due to natural causes may not be much of a stigma for many prospective buyers, but a house in which a murder or, worse, multiple murders occurred may prove to be too much for many buyers to stomach. It took two and a half years for the Brentwood, California, house in which Nicole Brown Simpson was murdered to sell, in an up-scale neighborhood in which houses were on the market an average of three months before being sold. After such a long time, the house was sold at a deep discount and the new owner invested even more money to completely remodel the façade so that the house bore no resemblance to its former self and was completely camouflaged from nosy tourists and curiosity-seekers.

In California, state law says that a real estate agent does not have to disclose a death that occurred in the house more than three years before the sale, although most agents agree that it is better to disclose all deaths, no matter how long ago they occurred, if the buyer asks. Pennsylvania has no laws governing stigmatized properties, but the commonwealth's Sellers Property Disclosure Statement requires sellers to disclose any "material defect" that might affect the value of the property. Of course, the definition of "material defect" is subject to interpretation. Is a ghost in any way defective? How could a ghost possibly be "material"?

In Massachusetts and Connecticut real estate agents are under no obligation to voluntarily disclose properties that may have been stigma-tized by murders, suicides, allegations of ghosts, or other potential stig-mas, but they must answer as truthfully and completely as possible if their clients specifically ask whether or not the property is stigmatized.

But what happens if you unknowingly purchase a house that is stigmatized, specifically by virtue of its being haunted? Do you have any legal recourse that allows you to back out of the deal or get your money back?

A 1990 court case in New York gives an affirmative answer to both questions. Jeffrey and Patrice Stambovsky paid Helen Ackley a $32,500 down payment on the $650,000 Hudson River Valley Victorian mansion Ackley was selling. In a casual conversation with a local architect, the Stambovskys discovered that the house was reputed to be haunted. More than reputed: Ackley herself had spent years promoting her house as a haunted hangout, and the house had been written about in many local and national publications.

In the 1997 Reader's Digest article "Our Haunted House on the Hudson," Ackley said that the mansion in Nyack was home to at least three ghosts dating from as far back as the Revolutionary War. There was a woman who wore a red cloak and was regularly seen on the stairs, a bewigged sailor, and an elderly man who seated himself suspended 4 feet above the living room floor. Ackley said that the ghosts were not harmful or malicious, but were, instead, "thoroughly entertaining." The house was also one of five listed on a haunted walking tour of Nyack.

Despite such ghostly hoopla, the Stambovskys, who lived out of town, did not know the house was haunted when they paid their down payment, nor had Ackley told them. When they found out, the couple demanded their money back and wanted to break the deal. Ackley refused, saying that they had agreed to purchase the house "as is." Both parties ended up in court. A lower court found in favor of Ackley but an appeal to the Appellate Division of the New York State Supreme Court reversed that earlier decision and found in favor of the Stambovskys.

Justice Israel Rubin explained the decision this way:

> A very practical problem arises with respect to the discovery of a paranormal phenomenon: "Who you gonna call?" as a title song to the movie Ghostbusters asks. Applying the strict rule of caveat emptor to a contract involving a house possessed by poltergeists conjures up visions of a psychic or medium routinely accompanying the structural engineers and Terminix

Embedded with the Paranormal Paramilitary
Riding with Mediums, Spirit Seekers, and Ghost Hunters
134

man on an inspection of every home subject to a contract of sale.

Whether the source of the spectral apparitions seen by defendant seller are parapsychic or psychogenic, having reported their presence in both a national publication and in the local press, defendant is estopped to deny their existence, and, as a matter of law, the house is haunted.

The Stambovskys got their money back and high-tailed it out of Nyack.

Another couple in Pennsylvania wanted to be released from their sales agreement to buy a house because they had heard that there were ghosts in the area—not the house, specifically, only the area. The owners of the house said they had never had any paranormal experiences in the house but, even so, added a "ghost inspection clause" in the contract that gave the buyers 10 days to conduct such a project—to no avail: The buyers pulled out of the deal.

Stigmatized properties are sometimes also called "psychologically impacted houses," and may be the bane of real estate brokers. Joseph Coleman and James Larson, two business professors from Wright State University in Dayton, Ohio, studied more than 100 psychologically impacted houses for their 2001 *Journal of Real Estate Practice and Education* article "Psychologically Impacted Houses." They found that such houses take as much as 50 percent longer on average to sell than normal homes, and that they sell at an average of 2.4 percent less.

But not every buyer is freaked by the idea of a haunted house. Some want to own one, as evidenced by the ads on eBay and other places. In 2004 a woman in Eugene, Oregon, ran an ad in The Register-Guard newspaper to sell her house and was careful to list, in addition to the bedrooms, baths, and formal dining room, one "resident ghost." She had several people come to view the house precisely because it was haunted.

Then there were the Schaibles of Fanwood, New Jersey, who, as they toured the attic of an 111-year-old Victorian house, asked the seller if it had ghosts. It did.

"We said we kind of think of it as a positive thing," Craig Schaible said.

The couple paid the owner's asking price and moved into the house in spring 2001. The stories about the house made it "completely more valuable," Schaible said. Their second night in the new house, with their belongings piled up everywhere, made it clear to the Schaibles that some other entity was sharing their house with them. Craig got up that night and walked into the 12-foot-wide main hallway. A heavy Civil War musket that had been leaning against the wall suddenly launched itself across the hall, landing at Craig's feet. That gave Schaible second thoughts about the appeal of living in a haunted house.

Schaible started literally talking to the walls. "I said, 'Hey, I live here, I pay the mortgage, and I don't need this scaring me out of my mind in the middle of the night.' I ranted for about an hour or so and sat around for a while," Schaible said.

After that, things quieted down, and the Schaibles heard strange voices and saw ghostly figures in the house only occasionally. Were they still scared?

"No," Craig Schaible said. "You have to live there to understand. It's not like a rattling of chains go bump in the night." The ghosts visited "so fast that it's over before you know it."

I am a lover of old houses and have always imagined owning some sprawling old Victorian mansion or a simple, austere New England saltbox house, but not until I started writing these books did I ever give thought to the fact that they might be haunted. That is something to consider. Visiting haunted houses was one thing, but living with ghosts, even Casper-style ghosts, was quite another. The next time I'm house-hunting, I'll be sure to ask the agent about ghosts, but, just to be on the safe side, I think I'll bring my dowsing rods along.

CHAPTER 13

GHOSTS IN THE ASYLUM

There are many spooky stories about Athens, Ohio, a place the British Society for Psychical Research recognizes as one of the most haunted places in the world, and a community profiled on Fox Family Channel's World's Scariest Places. Modern psychic researchers believe that the Athens area contains an extremely active vortex—that is, a portal between our world and the spirit world that allows spirits to easily travel between these realms. The Shawnee and ancient Native peoples before them knew the area as a center of strong energy, a place in which the spirits dwelt. For centuries, Native Shamans and healers sought guidance and inspiration from the spirits here, especially those atop Mount Nebo, the highest peak in the region, just more than 1,000 feet high. In the 19th century, an internationally renowned Spiritualist center was located upon Mount Nebo. There could be no better town for a ghosthunter to call home.

From the balcony of my apartment in Athens, I can see the twin Gothic towers of The Ridges rising above the trees on the other side of the Hocking River. The Ridges is the popular name given to the sprawling institution that was founded as the Athens Lunatic Asylum in 1874, and is now owned by Ohio University. At its peak in 1953, the asylum sheltered 1,749 patients and comprised 78 buildings spread over more than 1,000 acres. The hospital was mostly self-sufficient and had its own dairy, greenhouses, gardens, vineyards, and even a piggery.

Now it has ghosts.

The Ridges in Athens, Ohio.
Courtesy of John Kachuba.

The story most often told about The Ridges concerns the eerie figure of a woman imprinted upon the floor in one of the old abandoned wards, a woman who died there in 1978 under tragic and weird circumstances.

In the 1970s, the institution was known as the Athens Mental Health and Retardation Center and reflected the many advances in mental healthcare that had come about since the hospital's founding 100 years before. As a result of these advances, including new pharmaceuticals that allowed many patients to function in society, the huge buildings began to empty out. Many wards stood empty and abandoned.

On December 1, 1978, a 54-year-old patient who had the privilege of leaving the grounds as long as she returned in the evening went missing. After an intensive three-day hunt and a weeklong follow-up search, the woman had not turned up. Six weeks later, a maintenance man found the woman's body in a sunlit room on an abandoned third-floor ward. She was lying naked on the cement floor beneath tall windows, arms crossed and legs composed as if she had deliberately settled herself in that posture. Some accounts say that her clothes were found neatly folded in a pile on the window sill, others that she had dropped her clothes piece by piece out the window in an attempt to attract at-

The stain in the abandoned ward at The Ridges.
Courtesy of John Kachuba.

tention to her predicament, which was that she had become accidentally locked inside the abandoned ward. The coroner listed the cause of death as heart failure.

The woman's death is strange, but what is even stranger is the impression she left upon the floor. When her body was removed, a stain was left behind that clearly depicts her body. It is believed to have been created by the interaction of her own bodily chemicals with the bright sunlight that streamed through the windows during the weeks that she remained undiscovered. Maintenance workers say that trying to scrub the stain out of the cement only darkens it.

I had heard ridiculous tales of a curse attached to anyone who dared to touch the woman's image, including the story of an Ohio University coed who hung herself in her dorm after touching the figure. A newspaper reporter broke the news of her death to the astonished coed during an interview a few years after her supposed suicide. Despite the silly stories about the unfortunate patient, I snapped a photo of her image during a nocturnal ghost investigation at The Ridges conducted by the Ohio Exploration Society.

The ghosthunters had been invited to The Ridges by Barrett Skrypeck, a fine arts graduate student and teaching associate at Ohio University. I first met Barrett after I sent an e-mail to the university's fine arts department, looking for artists to convert my rusted-out 1987 Buick Skyhawk into a Ghosthuntermobile. (Such a car would be a unique way to advertise my books, I thought, and I wasn't risking much with my old clunker.) Barrett and a team of a half-dozen or so fine arts grad students went to work on the car and painted it all over with ghosts, demons, gravestones, haunted houses, and other assorted paranormal symbols.

The grad students' studios were located on an upper floor of The Ridges, in what had been one of the hospital wards. The university could not afford to renovate the floor, so maintenance men simply moved the hospital furniture out and let the artists in. Reminders of the patients who had once lived there were everywhere, especially in the religious and profane graffiti they had scratched into the exterior windowsills as they gazed out at the world, wishing for wings. Barrett's studio, as were most of the others, was a cramped, airless space that had been a patient's room. His artwork covered the walls, and every available inch of surface area was filled with art supplies.

Barrett had called the Ohio Exploration Society because of the ghosts roaming the decrepit halls of The Ridges.

"Several times, I've been sitting in my studio and, out of the corner of my eye, I'll see a figure glide past the door," Barrett told me. "When I get up to see who it is, no one is there."

The final-straw ghost for Barrett was the one he saw in the men's room. As he entered the lavatory he saw a man in a black coat reflected in the long mirror above the sinks. The position of the image in the mirror indicated that the man was already in the restroom, but when Barrett entered, he found himself alone in the room. The man could not have left the room without Barrett's knowledge, as there was only one door, and Barrett had just come in through it.

"I got the hell out of there quick," Barrett said.

As you can imagine, I accepted Barrett's invitation to join the investigation in a heartbeat.

I arrived early at The Ridges the night of the investigation. Standing outside the locked doors I looked up and saw the lights on in the tower windows where the studios were located. Against the night sky the shadowed turret with its lighted windows looked to be something out of an old Dracula movie. The Ridges is an isolated complex, cut off from the rest of the university by the river and the high ridge itself, so the parking lot was empty, except for my Ghosthuntermobile. It was a moonless night, and if anyone, or anything, was waiting in the shadows beneath the towers, I couldn't tell.

After a few minutes, a car pulled up, and three men and a woman got out and approached me. This was the Ohio Exploration Society (OES), headed by Jason Robinson. The other investigators were Jason Colwell, Misty Jones, and Abraham Bartlett. They were all, I guessed, in their mid- to late 20s and had driven down from Columbus. I was particularly pleased when they showed me the copy of Ghosthunting Ohio that they had in the car and had been reading on their way to Athens. They didn't know I would be at the investigation, so they weren't simply trying to impress me by reading my book; I loved these guys.

Barrett arrived, along with his wife, Becky, and Howie* from the university's maintenance department, who would act as something of a guide for our group and would unlock doors that weren't supposed to be unlocked. We all headed upstairs to the artists' studios.

The OES crew, each of them wearing shirts emblazoned with the group's name and logo, assembled their equipment on a table in an area the students had set up as a makeshift lounge. The room was done up in a Modern Goodwill motif and furnished with hideous orange upholstered chairs oozing their stuffing out of various rips and tears, an old battered TV, a small bookcase, and a weird assortment of decorative items hanging on the walls, including a collection of different-colored teddy bears and the naked torso of a doll, whose face had been garishly painted a la KISS's Gene Simmons and whose chest bore a crude pentacle. Artists, I thought. Go figure.

The lounge was situated in one of the building's towers and it was through its long narrow windows that I had seen the light from down below. Unlike the rest of us, Howie was an Athens native and had actually known some of the patients who were housed in the building when it

Embedded with the Paranormal Paramilitary
Riding with Mediums, Spirit Seekers, and Ghost Hunters
142

was in use as a hospital. He was decked out in a ball cap, denim jacket, and jeans with a silver belt buckle the size of a dinner plate.

"This area right here," he said, "used to be the patient's day room. You could see them looking out the windows, just wandering around here. I knew one of them, a family friend, maybe a distant relative, I don't know, named Hazel. My family used to visit her and I'd come along."

Howie walked over to the window and stood looking out at the parking lot down below, washed in yellow light from a single lamppost. He jingled the large ring of keys he wore on his belt, and then turned back to us.

"Hazel died several years ago, but she's never left this building. I know. I've seen her. Sometimes I'd be working outside and I'll look up and there she is, big as life, standing behind the windows, watching me."

"How do you know it was Hazel and not one of the artists?" I asked.

"Well, first it's because I knew her. I know what she looks like. Second, she was a different lady. Large. Red hair. She stood out in a crowd."

"Did you ever see her inside the building?" I said.

"Yes," Howie said, "I saw her standing in the doorway to what used to be the patient's activities room, wearing a yellow dress. There's plenty going on here, I'll tell you. Late at night, I'll be here by myself and I'll hear doors opening and closing, footsteps, that kind of thing. And I don't drink on the job," Howie added, even though I hadn't asked.

The OES investigators had unpacked their equipment and had laid it all out on the table. Jason Robinson explained to me how his group would conduct its investigation. A tall, thin guy wearing an OES T-shirt and navy ball cap turned backwards, Jason held a video camcorder in his hand while he spoke.

"First, we'll walk through the building and get an idea of its layout. We especially want to see the areas where people have reported something happening. Then we'll set up a few cameras on tripods in those areas and run tape for a while, see what happens. We'll also leave some tape recorders in other areas and see if we can pick up any EVPs." I had done my homework and knew that EVPs were electronic voice phenomena—recordings of voices, supposedly spirit voices that were captured on tape although inaudible to the people in the room at that time. "Every so often, we'll go around and check out the equipment, make sure everything is running right," Jason said.

As we stood talking, I noticed that more people were congregating in the lounge. Some of the other artists whose studios were in the building had joined us, accompanied by friends they had invited along. There were close to two dozen people. Some of them were sipping beer, a commodity easily found among the artists. The investigation was rapidly taking on the complexion of a frat party.

"A lot of people," I said to Jason. "Will that affect your investigation?"

He frowned. "It might, but it's a big building. Maybe if we split up, it might work out better."

It seemed, however, that everyone wanted to go along on the initial tour led by Howie. I couldn't blame them, because the abandoned wards of the hospital were off limits to the public, yet were the source of much local speculation about ghosts. There was no way, however, that any respectable ghost would put in an appearance as this rowdy, beer-swilling circus tromped through the dark and dusty halls.

The OES team, to their credit, remained aloof to the shenanigans of the others and tried their best to conduct a serious investigation. For my part, whenever Howie led us into yet another gloomy hall, I separated myself from the others as best I could in order to soak up as much of the environment as possible. This had been my modus operandi in countless other visits to haunted locations, simply to find a quiet place where I could be alone, open and receptive to whatever may reside in that place. It wasn't easy to employ that method that night, but I tried.

I wandered in and out of dark rooms without a flashlight and wondered what had taken place in them. Had they been patients' rooms? Were they treatment rooms? Nurses' stations? Most of the furnishings were long gone, but every so often, I would stumble across an old chair, cabinet, or other small piece of furniture. I could hear the others walking in the hall, sometimes see the beams of their flashlights bouncing over the floor, as I stood quietly in a room, waiting. No positive emotions emanated from that place. Locked in their dementia, these poor patients had suffered. Hundreds of them lay buried in two cemeteries

Embedded with the Paranormal Paramilitary
Riding with Mediums, Spirit Seekers, and Ghost Hunters
144

on the hospital's grounds, many of them beneath stone markers that bore only a number. The reason for this anonymity seems to have been to spare family members the indignity and embarrassment of publicly revealing that a relative had been committed to the Lunatic Asylum. It was sad to think that these people, who suffered in life through no fault of their own and endured horrific "treatments" in an attempt to cure them of their maladies, would lie beneath the green grass still spurned by humanity. If ever there were a place where lost souls clamored for recognition, for dignity, for peace, it was those cemeteries.

I could hear the voices of the others growing fainter, so I trailed behind them as Howie led us all up a flight of stairs to the ward in which the woman had died in 1978. We entered the small room where the body had been found and I wondered once again how it was that she was unable to make her presence known through the tall windows to rescuers outside. The thought struck me that perhaps she wasn't looking to be saved. Maybe it was simply her time to die and she knew it. Accepted it. Flashlights played across her image, still clearly visible upon the dusty concrete floor; the OES team shot some video and still photography.

Howie took us up to the attic. The space below the sloping roof of the building was enormous and was divided into several large rooms, separated by brick walls. Arched doorways led from one room into another. Oddly, the floor was covered with a layer of soft dirt, rather than dust, and none of us, Howie included, could account for its origin. We wandered around in the attic, poking into nooks and little rooms. The usual wiring and ductwork typical of an institutional building snaked through the attic, but there was nothing else up there. Jason's flashlight did find evidence that someone had discovered the attic a long time ago: As he entered another long room, the light picked up some graffiti spray-painted on the brick wall in 2-foot-high letters. The graffiti read: "July 11.1960 Kennedy for President." I had been only 10 years old when some unknown Democrat painted the slogan in the attic. Where no one would ever see it.

From the attic we walked all the way down to the basement, a dark and dirty warren of rooms and tunnels. After so much trekking through the building, the most boisterous of the group were starting to flag and some had broken off from the group to find their way back to the comfort of the artists' lounge. The remainder of us explored the basement, probing through piles of old junk, including sections of the hospital's original wrought iron fences and gates. In a tiny brick room Howie showed us a cistern in which he said one of the doctors had kept a pet alligator. Howie didn't know why.

We emerged from the basement and went back upstairs to the artists' studios. There, the OES team decided where they would place their cameras and tape recorders. They set up a video camera on a tripod in a section of abandoned offices, and another in an ominous room on the same floor as the studios, a room in which blue ceramic tiles completely covered the walls. Drains were set in the floor. Metal jets protruded from the walls, maybe for gas or oxygen, no one knew. The room reminded me of an old-fashioned surgical suite, but it could just as easily have been a kitchen. A couple of people in the group said that they felt some sort of "presence" in that room. Another camera and tape recorder were set up in the lavatory where Barrett had seen his ghost.

Then we waited. This is one aspect of ghosthunting that none of the popular television programs about ghosthunters ever seem to show—the boring wait for something to happen. Often, nothing ever does happen. Ghosthunters live for the momentary glimpse of something unusual on a video monitor, or for a few seconds of unidentifiable sound on a tape recording, and it can take many hours of investigation to produce those few results. Ghosts don't respond well to command performances and are notorious for making themselves known when all the cameras, tape recorders, and other monitoring equipment are already turned off or removed. Still, it is quite a rush when something does make itself known.

Every now and then, Jason or one of the members of his team would make the rounds and check the equipment. Sometimes, they would take still photos as they went. I accompanied Jason and Abe Bartlett on one such check. I asked them how often they had encountered ghosts on their investigations and, though they admitted that it was pretty unusual to actually see an apparition, they had collected a good number of EVPs from some of the places they had investigated. Although a relatively new group, the Ohio Exploration Society had already conducted investigations into dozens of haunted cemeteries, houses, hospitals, restaurants,

Native American burial mounds (fairly common in Ohio), schools, and other assorted haunts.

Nothing unusual happened that night at The Ridges. The partygoers quickly tired of the whole thing and left, no doubt seeking the livelier haunts of the Court Street bars catering to Ohio University students. That left Barrett and Becky, Howie, a couple of die-hard artists, the OES team, and me to close down the investigation. Around 1 a.m. we packed up the equipment and called it a night.

It takes quite a while for an investigative team to analyze the film, photos, and tape recordings that are made during the investigation, so it was a couple of weeks before I again heard from Jason. Apparently, I had been wrong in thinking that nothing had happened that night. Although we never felt their presence, the ghosts of The Ridges certainly knew we were there and did their best to communicate with us. The OES team had recorded two EVPs. In a room that had formerly been a padded cell, Jason recorded someone yelling on his digital audio recorder. As the group came up from the basement, Misty Jones's microcassette recorder picked up a whispered voice saying, "Would you help us?"

Who are these ghosts? How can they be helped? After all those poor spirits endured when they were flesh and blood, it would be a blessing if someone could reach them and set them free.

CHAPTER 14

LIVING IN FEAR ENDS

M ichael Jones was 5 years old the first time a ghost tried to touch him.

His mother, Denice, was downstairs when she heard her son screaming; a shrill, animal-like shriek that would instantly stop cold the heart of any parent. She ran upstairs to find Michael lying on the floor of his bedroom, tightly curled into a ball, his pale face a contorted mask of terror. The boy told her that a man had been in his room and had tried to touch him on the shoulder. Denice was stabbed by fear as she thought that an intruder might have broken into her house. She grabbed the nearest thing to a weapon she could find—one of Michael's metal toy trucks—and searched the house, warily opening closet doors, ready to bash the interloper with the truck. There was no intruder.

She went back to Michael's room, calmed the boy down, and then went back downstairs. She hadn't been there but a few minutes when Michael started screaming again. She raced back upstairs and found her son in tears, trembling. The man had come back, Michael told her, and he described him to her: an old man, pale white, surrounded by a blinding light. Again, he had tried to touch the boy.

This time Denice bundled Michael and her older son Kenny into her car and drove to her mother's house. Her mother would know what to do, Denice thought. While she was talking with her parents at the house, Michael wandered into another room. He began screaming yet again. Pointing a shaky finger at a framed photo hanging on the wall, Michael identified the man in the picture as the man who had been in his room. The man was his great-grandfather Pierce, dead for many years.

"Michael started screaming, 'This is the guy who tried to touch me,'" Denice said, as I spoke with her in the study of her Manchester, Connecticut, home. "My father tried to talk with Michael and told him, 'It's okay, this is your great-grandfather. He won't hurt you," but there was a problem with him saying that. What Michael heard was that, because his great-grandfather was good, he [could] open up, and started talking to everyone and everything that would come in."

By "everyone" and "everything" Denice meant ghosts and other entities.

"I was thinking that no one was going to tell him that there could be something negative that could come in," Denice continued. "We were not going to scare the kid. He just opened up some door and that's when Michael started having a lot of problems."

That's putting it mildly.

During the next few years, Michael was subjected to horrific paranormal experiences that would have completely broken a healthy and strong-willed adult. As Denice related the story to me during our conversation, and as she had done in her book, *The Other Side*, it seems to me nothing short of miraculous that Michael survived; he was 18 years old when I interviewed Denice for this book. Grandpa Pierce continued to visit him, Michael now realizing he was a friendly spirit, but other spirits, considerably less benevolent, had haunted Michael as well. Balls of light flew through his room, and frightening voices emanated from them. A shadow person loomed over his bed at night, trying to smother him. Something with a bloody, gashed head slashed his skin and he frequently awoke with strange handprints, welts, and bruises covering his body. Often, he was "scratched and slapped right in front of us," as Denice described it. Michael's health was suffering. He was not sleeping well, was bruised and battered, and lived in constant fear.

"Michael comes from a gifted family," Denice said. "My great-great-grandfather was a medicine man and my mother can sense spirits. She gets freezing cold, to the bone, when spirits are around. I don't see spirits all the time. I can feel them, I know when they're here, I can hear them, and I hear my spirit guides a lot. Michael sees spirits like he sees you and me, 24 hours a day.

"When my son started having it all happen to him I didn't want it to be paranormal because I didn't want him to go through what I went through of being afraid. As a mother, I needed to make sure it was not something else."

Denice took Michael to several doctors—ophthalmologists, neurologists, psychiatrists—all of whom gave the boy a clean bill of health. He was not "seeing things"; the events were not "in his head." With nowhere left to go, Denice turned to the Catholic Church for help, but was turned down. She wrote to famed paranormal investigators and demonologists Ed and Lorraine Warren, but never received a reply from them.

Denice began to feel as though she were fighting for her son's life all alone. She decided to move out of the haunted house, but was demoralized to find that the new house was even worse. It wasn't the houses that were haunted, she realized; it was her son. Worse, she understood that not only was Michael contacted by ghosts, but by demonic spirits that were trying to kill him for reasons known only to them.

"I actually think Michael had a demonic case the whole time," Denice remembered. "He seems to pull in the negative really bad, I guess some people do. These things seem to really want Michael, I don't understand why. I think, in the future we're going to know that."

Denice finally found help for Michael in the form of Bishop Carey, from a breakaway Catholic church in Monroe, Connecticut, who performed an exorcism on the boy. Perhaps of even greater help were the ghosts of Grandpa Pierce and of Justin Kelly, Michael's best friend, who had been killed in a car accident. These ghosts acted more like guardian angels as they protected Michael from demonic attacks; to this day, Michael still talks with his spirit friend Justin.

Denice explained that up until a year or two ago, Michael continued to live with constant fear, although the attacks had ceased. She could not let him out of her sight without something happening to him. Michael could not go into another room to get a soda without Denice being there. When he showered, Denice would sit in the bathroom with her back turned, waiting for him. Much of his education was homeschooling because he was always exhausted from sleepless nights and unable to

Denice and Michael Jones.
Courtesy of Denice Jones.

function in the classroom—still he graduated from high school with high honors and now holds a job as a computer technician. He continues to sleep with the lights on.

"What happened that helped him overcome his fears?" I asked her.

"He had an experience that a lot of people are going to think is off the wall, really nuts," Denice said. "He went out of his body and something grabbed him by the neck and went down through the window and into the ground here, right in the front yard. Michael said that he found himself standing on this ledge and that there was an entity that he could not see, but he knew it was there, and he knew that he had known that entity for many, many years. He said that he was watching people being torn apart down below him and the thing said to him, 'Are you afraid, Michael?' and Michael said that he wasn't afraid, but he didn't know why not. It was almost as though he was comfortable with this thing and he knew he was all right. The entity said, 'Then why are you afraid over there?' Michael thought about it for a moment and the next thing he knew he popped back into his body, jumped up and ran for me to tell me what had happened. His first words were, 'Mom, I just went to Hell.'"

Denice recounted this hair-raising story to me calmly and coolly, indicating to me that these kinds of events were not at all surprising occurrences in Michael's life.

"It was a complete change for Michael," Denice said. "He was frightened to death, and I mean to death, and then all of a sudden, he's not anymore. Michael goes upstairs by himself, he takes a shower by himself; it's very strange. It was like a night and day thing with him."

Michael still sees ghosts, every day, all the time, and he has also developed new paranormal abilities. In addition to his recently acquired talent for stepping out of his body—what parapsychologists call an out-of-body experience, or OOB for short—Michael has been having visions. In one of them he saw a police officer attacked by four men. The problem with Michael's visions, Denice said, was that so far, they did not match up with any actual event, and neither Denice nor Michael knew if they pertained to the present, the past, or the future. In that respect, they more closely resembled really bad dreams than visions.

Still, Michael has learned to deal with the fear. "Before, he didn't know why it was happening to him. He didn't like it much at all. But now, as he's gotten older, he's thinking that he wants to help people. He wants to go out and investigate," Denice said.

On the advice of psychic medium John Holland, Denice contacted Journey Within, a Spiritualist church in Wayne, New Jersey, to help Michael understand his abilities and learn better how to control them. If the process goes well for Michael in New Jersey, Denice said she would consider sending him to Arthur Findlay College in England, whose website advertises Findlay as "The World's Foremost College for the Advancement of Spiritualism and Psychic Sciences."

"These are big changes for Michael," I said, "and for you. How has all of this affected your life?"

"I've been happy and living my life because before, I couldn't leave him in the house alone. I couldn't go far away. It seemed like every time

I left, I would get those calls and I would have to run home because Michael was being attacked or something else was happening."

"And it's given you more time to devote to L.I.F.E.," I said, referring to the Living In Fear Ends foundation Denice established in 1995.

"Yes, it has."

"Tell me how and why you set up L.I.F.E."

"I did it because when things first started I couldn't find help for Michael. I didn't know where to go. I didn't understand it. I knew we had these abilities, but I didn't have the ability of knowing how to get rid of it. I just knew they lived with us. They were there. It was getting scary. So, I founded L.I.F.E. because of that. I figured if someone needed help, I'd be damned if I'd let them be harassed, not only by the spirits, but by people who either want to milk them out of everything they own, or just want publicity."

"What does L.I.F.E. actually do?" I asked.

Denice explained that she had associations with paranormal investigators all across the country, people who she said were "pros, good investigators knowledgeable about demonology, as well as earthbound spirits." People who were troubled by ghosts and other spirit entities would first contact Denice through her L.I.F.E. website and she would correspond with them.

"I can figure out who's telling the truth and who's not telling the truth and who needs what kind of help," she said. "I'll contact someone in their state, in their area, to go investigate it, and if it's something they do not know how to get rid of, I will find that help—the clergy, whatever. I'll link you up to what you need and I'll make sure that you're okay and I'll contact you after to make sure the investigators were okay and so forth."

When I asked Denice how many people had contacted her L.I.F.E. foundation, she said that she had stopped counting at 11,000, and "that was, believe it or not, years and years and years ago." She continues to receive as many as 30 e-mails every day from people seeking help. "I didn't know that many people had paranormal problems. I'm only one person. I'd be up all night, trying to help these people."

Denice is more than simply a paranormal intermediary, however. "Every single day I'm on the computer working with the L.I.F.E. foundation, helping families. I've got a lot of cases. I do not go out on investigations by myself, although I know I could. You should never go without somebody else. I like all the investigation companies and I just choose one and go out with them and watch them work. I get to know them better that way."

With all that Denice and Michael have been through over the years, they have learned how to help others with similar problems. "People feel comfortable with me and I know what that is when you're going through something like this. You just can't do anything about it. It's almost like you're being raped, it's that same kind of feeling," Denice said.

As Michael matures and learns more about his psychic abilities, he may be able to help his mother in her work with L.I.F.E. "Michael's gotten older and he wants to go out and investigate," Denice said. "He's thinking now that he wants to help people. He's not afraid anymore like he used to be. He just wants to help."

CHAPTER 15

GHOST BE GONE

It's one thing to run into a ghost while doing an investigation in a haunted location, but what do you do when the ghost is in your own home and you absolutely, positively want it gone? Who you gonna call?

You might call Drude Clark, a certified medical hypnotist, and Dr. Susan Benedict, a chiropractor. For several years the California duo, better known as Ghost Be Gone, has been ridding homes, offices—any personal spaces—of unwanted spirits they call "densities." Although the team prefers to work in person at a haunted location, they are also quite capable of clearing a space remotely, without ever setting foot on the premises.

"Both methods are quite successful," said Drude, during a conversation I had with the women. "We use different approaches on site than we do when working remote. Essentially, we clear, or remove, densities that are not in harmony with the soul purpose of those who inhabit the space, including their own bodies. A density is the word I am using here to explain how we sense it, whether caused by a discarnate—a ghost, an evil entity, or one's own trash—high volumes of negativity and perversity generated by a person or space."

Drude and Susan met during a La Chance Emotional Release training session. The La Chance method involves physical bodywork—pats, sounds, and verbal encouragement—to free up energy that is spent in keeping painful memories and experiences outside our fields of consciousness. The freed energy can then be used in positive and productive ways. The women struck up a friendship and, when one of Susan's clients asked her to do a house clearing, Susan consulted with Drude and their partnership was born. The women further trained with the late Dr. Irene Hickman, an osteopathic physician who also discovered how to incorporate hypnosis into her practice in order to better serve her patients' health needs.

"In the Hickman method, people work in pairs," Drude explained. "One person is under a state of hypnosis and the other person acts like a guide or facilitator that invites the energetic, whether it's a ghost, discarnate, entity, or some other form, to come forward and to speak through the person without causing her harm in any way."

In one of their most interesting cases, the women were asked to clear an Italian villa that had been having problems with negative energies. Drude was the facilitator as Susan entered a hypnotic state.

"I sent my consciousness to Italy, to the villa," said Susan. "I found a closet in one of the upstairs rooms that I felt really had to be cleared out. Whatever was in there was not the energy the people living there wanted in their house. It turned out that in that closet were stored full-length fur coats that had belonged to someone who had passed on. We recommended that they clear out the closet, to do it posthaste, get it out of the house."

"Once they did that, the house was fine," Drude added.

"How exactly did you clear the villa?" I asked.

"The method lies in our intention with a shift of consciousness on our part," Drude said. "When you set an intention it's like throwing a switch a little bit. You change your vibratory field. You just move over a click or two and go into it. You set your intention to be in the field with that ghost, or discarnate, the essence of a departed person that is present in another dimension. You have the mindset of meeting that vibration in a very respectful way, more like an inquiry: 'How can we help you? What are you doing here and why are you stuck?'"

Susan said, "When you set the intention you're calling on the forces that be to come in and help you. That's how I always think of it because I'm asking that my intentions be met, or at least be respected. I think that causes kind of a chain of events. If you're clear before you go in, I think you receive."

In another case, a woman who was afraid of her husband's dog contacted Susan and Drude. She and her husband had several cats and dogs, but one dog in particular, a German Shepard mix, was not seeing eye to eye with the woman. The Ghost Be Gone team went to the woman's house.

"We found an energy, you could call it a density, I guess," Susan said. "It was something buried in the backyard, or something that had happened in the back yard."

"The hallway inside the house was also really bad," said Drude. "Later on, we found out that someone who had lived there previously used to have temper tantrums there. You know, he would put his fist through the wall.

"I think as a by-product of that, the dog had some kind of fear, and, yes, it did relate somehow to the back yard. But I just talked to that dog and told it everything would be okay, and not to be afraid. I remember holding the dog's head, talking to it, petting it. I wasn't thinking I was doing anything special but after that visit, the dog and the homeowner, where there before had been all this negative interaction, that dog became her favorite pet."

"It was a complete reversal," added Susan. "The homeowners found that an animal had died and had been buried right on that spot in the backyard. I think that was part of what was spooking the dog."

"Maybe we cleared away a little doggie ghost," said Drude. "Animals are such a reflection of what's going on with people."

I said, "There is a sentence on your Ghost Be Gone website that reads, 'Releasing the old vibrations can be compared to taking out the garbage.' Have you ever had any cases in which the garbage just didn't want to leave?"

"Whether we're working with people or a discarnate, we invite whatever we find to rise to a higher plane," said Susan. "But sometimes it may be unwilling to go. Demonic energy, for example, has a lot more 'oomph' to it."

"We had one case in which the entity didn't want to leave. It wanted the house to be dead," Drude said. "It was causing heart attacks and other problems. This energy was on a mission. Sometimes, we run into that kind of thing, something that was created by, for lack of a better term, black magick. If there's enough hate behind a thought it can create something like that. I think that's how voodoo works. We did get it to move on, though, we did change it. Later on, we found out that the history of heart attacks and all the other problems subsequent to that had cleared up.

"We've encountered some entities that definitely had a lot more spunk. They could be a little frightening. That's when we make sure we have a facilitator because you don't want to be in that type of environment by yourself. That's why we work together. You don't want to be ungrounded when you're wrestling with something that has a will."

In my research I had spoken with many mediums and ghostbusters who were actively involved in convincing spirits to move on to the next realm, to "go to the light," as many in this field say. As have Drude and Susan, some of them have run up against stubborn spirits who, for whatever reasons, resist eviction. One such spirit gave medium and ghosthunter, Psychic Sonya of Cleveland, Ohio, a battle.

It began with hot water suddenly gushing from the faucets at night, unexplainable rushes of cold wind, and exploding light bulbs, but Sonya knew beyond doubt that the Main Street Café on the Medina, Ohio, town square was haunted when she received the impression of a man sitting on the stairs watching her do a Tarot card reading.

"I kept seeing the letter D," Sonya said, as we spoke on the phone, "and eventually his name came to me. Daniel."

Sonya didn't know why the man was there or what he wanted, until she heard that human bones had been found in the coffee shop next door during a renovation project and that the owner of the shop had discarded them.

"All I can say is that you never desecrate human remains. It's a bad thing to do, really bad juju," Sonya said.

It was in the basement of the 120-year-old building where most of the ghostly activity took place. I had visited the Main Street Café before speaking with Sonya. One of the waitresses there told me about another waitress who had set the tables downstairs, lit all the candles, then left the room. When she came back only a few minutes later, every place setting had been turned upside down—every knife, fork, and spoon.

But that was only part of the haunting. Sonya told me that Daniel had started acting up. In a bad way.

"He seemed to be attaching himself to Frank*, the dishwasher," Sonya said. "Frank used to wear this old Marine compass on a chain around his neck. One day, it suddenly shattered into pieces. He had worn it for years and had never had any problem. Then light bulbs started exploding and Frank cut his hand when he went to change one of them. He was becoming so annoyed by the ghost that at one point, he said he would like to send it back to hell. No sooner had he said that, than he fell down the basement stairs, injuring his neck and shoulder."

Sonya brought in two friends to help her get rid of Daniel. One was a psychic investigator, the other a healer. They set up a video camera and tape recorder. Although they did not record any images, they did record an EVP, an electronic voice phenomenon.

"There was nothing but silence on the tape, then clear as a bell, a man's voice said, 'Go away.' I knew then Daniel would not go easily," Sonya said.

She continued her research and put together a plausible story for the spirit of Daniel. She said he came from Cleveland and was only in his 20s when he died, sometime around 1830. She doesn't know how he died, but she is sure he did not receive a proper burial. She believes the bones discovered in the wall next door belonged to Daniel and that his haunting is a result of the desecration exacted upon his final resting place.

Sonya said that she was interested in knowing the ghost's history only to the point that it would help her get rid of it. "I don't care what the ghost's story is," she said, "it's leaving. Ghosts are earthbound spirits. They are trapped here when, in fact, they need to move on. They're not healthy to have around, period. They have to go. Some of them don't even know they're dead, but once they understand that, they will move on. Others, like Daniel, are more stubborn and don't want to go."

Sonya was concerned about Frank. His coworkers told her that his personality was changing. He was becoming depressed, sometimes surly and angry. Sonya feared that Daniel was taking over.

Sonya conducted a healing ceremony at the restaurant with her two friends. She didn't give me the details, but did say that her team was able to free Frank from the ghost's influence. After the ceremony, Sonya and the healer, along with a photographer from the local newspaper who was on hand to cover the event, went into the alley near the wall where the bones had been found. There, she knelt in the snow and said the prayers of a Christian burial service and gave Daniel the rites that had been denied him so long ago. She looked up and saw a huge, bright cloud above the photographer's head.

"It was the angels, come to take Daniel away," she said. "He didn't want to go. I saw him kicking and screaming as the angels dragged him away."

CHAPTER 16

GHOSTS OF THE BATTLEFIELD

There is an aura over a battlefield, created by acts of privation, courage, and sacrifice that cannot be felt at other historical sites. A visitor to such a battlefield can never truly understand the travails of those who fought and died there, but one can feel an emotional tug, a spiritual pang of empathy at such places. Some say that there is more to that spiritual empathy than we can comprehend, and that the spirits of those who have died on the battlefield remain forever bound to it.

Fort Meigs in Perrysburg, Ohio, is one of those places.

During the War of 1812, General William Henry Harrison, newly appointed commander of the Northwest Army, was determined to thwart the British advance into what was then the Northwest Territory by establishing a log and earthen fort on a bluff overlooking the southern shore of the Maumee River in northwestern Ohio. The fort was a sprawling structure for its time, built to serve as a temporary supply depot and staging area for an American invasion of Canada. Approximately 2,000 men were sheltered in tents within the fort's perimeter and included U.S. Army regulars, militia from Ohio, Kentucky, Pennsylvania, and Virginia, and several companies of volunteers.

It was difficult to get a sense of that bustling activity on the day I visited the reconstructed fort. I was alone. There was no sound in the vast, open space enclosed by the wooden palisade, other than crickets sawing in the high grass and the wind whispering over the grounds. A solitary hawk floated high above the fort in a clear blue sky.

As I walked among the traverses—long, earthen berms taller than a man, thrown up as protection against incoming artillery rounds—the wind abated. There was only silence.

It was among these traverses one night that Virginia Pfouts, a volunteer at the fort, saw the dark shape of a man during a recent Garrison Ghost Walk. She had been dressed in 19th-century long dress and bonnet and carried a lantern as she conducted the tour.

"It was more of a silhouette," she said, during my visit to the fort. "I saw it in an area of the fort that the tour did not visit. There shouldn't have been anyone down there. I got closer and looked down another traverse to where the man had been. He was gone. None of the volunteers said they had been in that section that night. I know it wasn't one of the people on the tour. We count noses and keep a close watch on them so we don't lose anyone in the dark."

During the British sieges of Fort Meigs in May and July, 1813, American observers would stand upon the traverses. By watching how the smoke from British cannons across the river drifted on the wind, they could predict with a fair degree of accuracy where the projectile would hit and shout a warning to the soldiers in that area to duck for cover. It was dangerous work. A solid-shot cannonball could take away a man's head, or leave him standing for a few seconds with a bloody hole drilled through his chest big enough to look through. A "bomb bursting in air," as Francis Scott Key wrote during the same war, could pepper him with shrapnel or turn him into a human torch with flammable resins.

Could Virginia's specter have been the ghost of one of these unfortunate casualties?

"Some people have seen ghostly figures walking upon the traverses," said John Destatte, a volunteer at the fort with more than 13 years' experience. "There are certainly enough tragic stories from the fort's past that could account for the many ghost stories."

He told me how a detachment of Kentucky militia came to the aid of the besieged fort, captured a British gun battery across the river, and then fell into a trap set by "retreating" Indians. Those who were

A haunted blockhouse in Ft. Meigs, Perrysburg, Ohio.
Courtesy of John Kachuba.

not killed in battle were taken prisoner by the Indians and subjected to torture until Shawnee chief Tecumseh heard about it and put a halt to the tortures, all the while upbraiding as "women" the British officers who stood by and let it happen. Of the 800-man detachment, 650 were killed or captured.

"One of them was a captain," John said, "who had been seriously wounded by a musket ball that entered one temple and passed out through the other without killing him. The ball severed his optic nerve and the man was blinded. He wandered over the battlefield until the Indians killed and scalped him."

Indians are said to haunt the fort in addition to soldiers. Unbeknownst to General Harrison, the site had been previously used by Native Americans for several centuries. As American soldiers constructed the fort, human remains were unearthed. An entry from the 1813 diary of Captain Daniel Cushing reads:

> In almost every place where we have thrown up the earth we find human bones aplenty. Yesterday the fatigue party that were digging a trench in front of blockhouse No. 3 and 4 came upon a pile of bones where they took out 25 skulls in one pit....In walking around this garrison on the earth that has been thrown up it was like walking on the sea shore upon mussel shells, only in this case human bones.

It came as no surprise to hear both Virginia and John say that the area around blockhouse No. 3 was where most people reported unusual events. John talked about the woman and child sometimes seen peering from a second-floor window and the bluish-white light that had been seen floating in the dark near the blockhouse, and then drifting down the slope to the river.

"People who have seen it say that it is an Indian spirit, although they can't explain why they feel that way," he said.

Virginia has seen the light.

"It was as bright as a camera flash," she said, "only it lasted longer. A full four seconds, at least. It wasn't a camera. No one in our group was using one. There were no other lights that could have made the flash."

Virginia has had other experiences at blockhouse No. 3. One night, after she and some other volunteers had locked up the blockhouses and were returning to their cars in the parking lot, two police cruisers pulled up. The officers told her that the motion detectors in one of the blockhouses had been triggered. Something was inside.

"Sometimes there will be a false alarm," she said. "Maybe a mouse or something. I went back into the fort to check. The policemen didn't come with me."

She went to all the blockhouses, checked the locks, and found them all securely fastened. Then she came to blockhouse No. 3 with the steep traverse running close in front of it.

"I was standing at the door in the dark. I checked the lock. It was still locked. Suddenly, I heard the sound of a musket misfiring behind me, from up above the traverse. I whirled around but there was no one there."

"A musket?" I asked.

"I've heard that sound plenty of times during reenactments. I recognized it immediately."

Are the spirits of Fort Meigs still at war?

John said that some people have seen soldiers firing weapons. Virginia said that two women from Canada saw a ghostly gun crew working a cannon at the fort's Grand Battery at 3 a.m. I never did find out what the women were doing at the fort at 3 a.m. (Virginia did not feel that she should speak on their behalf, and no one could remember their full names or where they lived. Canada's a big country.)

I didn't see any ghosts at Fort Meigs, but I did find the melancholy gravestones of three officers killed there. The graves were not far from the soaring obelisk that memorializes the soldiers of Fort Meigs. Nor are they far from the cold spot—"refrigerator cold," Virginia called it—that some people have felt even in the brightest sunlight. Indians murdered one of the officers outside the fort. British artillery killed another as he conferred with General Harrison inside the fort, and the other, wounded at the Grand Battery, died from tetanus a few days later. Scores of the dead are buried in unmarked graves just outside the fort's main gate, and others lie in peace in an adjacent cemetery.

During the May 1813 siege, British troops managed to set up an artillery battery on the site now occupied by that cemetery. In a bloody attack, American troops overran the battery and knocked it out of commission. Apparently, that engagement rages on almost two hundred years later. People have heard the sounds of battle—fifes and drums, hoof beats—echoing from the site.

Virginia has heard a soldier walking beside her.

One evening she and some of the other volunteers were walking out from the visitors' center to their cars. She had parked her car in a different area removed from the others, and one of the volunteers asked her if she wanted to be escorted to her car. She said no, that she had her soldier walking beside her.

"Now, why in the world did I say that?" Virginia said. "It just came out. It was very strange. As I was walking to my car, I had the sense of someone else with me, and I heard a little metallic jingling accompanying me. It sounded like the rattling of a musket tool against a belt buckle. Whenever I stopped the sound stopped too."

She checked her haversack and her camera case, shaking them, to see if they were making the sound. They were not. Some time later, another volunteer said she had heard the same sound, only in a different part of the fort.

Virginia has felt the presence of an unseen person before. Once, when she was whitewashing the interior of blockhouse No. 1, she experienced an overwhelming sensation that someone was behind her, watching her. She turned to look, but there was no one there. Although she has never heard them herself, Pfouts says that some people have heard footsteps pacing the second floor of the blockhouse.

"None of this bothers me," she said. "There is nothing I fear at the fort."

But there were volunteers who refused to go to certain places within the fort after dark.

"In all my years here," John said, "I have never experienced anything unusual. Yet, people will tell me what they have felt or seen in a certain area of the fort and I'll research what happened there and say that makes sense."

"It really bugs me when people make up stories about what they've seen or heard at the fort," Virginia added. "It makes it so much harder for those of us who have really experienced these things to be believed.

"I believe the spirits of 1813 are still at the fort. It is paranormal. I don't know how else to explain it."

John and Virginia are certainly not alone when it comes to experiencing ghostly phenomena related to military engagements. Historical reenactors from all across the country have seen soldier ghosts, heard the ghostly echoes of drums and cannons, and smelled an elusive scent of gunpowder. It should come as no surprise that so many ghosts still muster on battlefields. These places are saturated with psychic impressions left as a result of the incredible emotional and physical turbulence experienced by the soldiers who fought and died at them. Such impressions could last a long time. Perhaps forever.

One theory about ghosts is that they are perceived only by people who are sensitive to them, people who are psychically attuned to the ghost's time period and circumstances. This theory goes a long way towards explaining why reenactors, people who live and breathe a historical period long gone, so often report ghost stories during reenactments. This is especially true for the thousands of reenactors who bring to life once again the bloody battles of the Civil War.

Antietam. Shiloh. Gettysburg. These names mean something to even the poorest student of American history, as they should, considering their significance in the course of the Civil War, and also considering the sheer carnage left behind when the smoke cleared. Grown men wept then at those places as they still do today.

Gettysburg may be the most haunted of all Civil War battlefields. Its ghosts are certainly well known, made popular by the books of Mark Nesbitt, a former National Parks Service ranger and historian, and the various ghost tours of the town and battlefield operated by Mark and others. The very first person to see a ghost on the Gettysburg battlefield was John Burns, a 70-year-old War of 1812 veteran who lived in Gettysburg and joined the fight when Confederate troops entered the town in July 1863. One day, three or four years later, he rounded a tree in the woods to find himself facing a Confederate soldier, who promptly vanished. Since that time, many people have had contact with the paranormal at Gettysburg, including countless reenactors.

One such reenactor was Private Cass, from the 42nd Pennsylvania Volunteers, who reported how some members of his unit had encountered a brush with the paranormal at Gettysburg at an old covered bridge known as Sachs Bridge. It was across that bridge that defeated Confederates began their retreat from Gettysburg.

"Back in June a few of us decided to go to Sachs Bridge and check out the claims that it is haunted," Cass said. "It was close to dusk, and as they approached the bridge, in uniform, they thought they saw a lady in period dress on the other side. Advancing to talk to her, she disappeared in front of them. It doesn't end there. The three ladies that were with them began to be overcome and wept uncontrollably. They retreated to the vehicles.

"Meanwhile, the guys continued to check out the covered bridge. As they walked they heard the sound of heel plates other than their own. When they turned around there was no one there. They decided to leave. As they reached the end of the bridge they heard ropes snapping. There were no ropes around anywhere."

Later research revealed that three Confederate deserters had been hung from the bridge. Had the reenactors heard the sounds of that grisly event replayed more than a century later?

A fair number of reenactors are women, and some of them have had ghostly encounters at historical sites. This is not surprising, because many researchers believe that women are generally more receptive to psychic phenomena than men. In theory then, a female reenactor might be even more likely to have a psychic battlefield experience than a male because of her gender as well as her strong affinity for the historical past.

Carole Julius and her husband, Dale, are reenactors with the 25th Massachusetts Volunteer Infantry, which is part of a reenactors' association known as the New England Brigade. They have made several trips to Gettysburg. On one such trip, Carole heard a troop of nonexistent soldiers marching by.

"My husband was walking up to Little Round Top, but I had decided to wait in the car," Carole told me. "I had the window rolled down and as I sat there I heard the clinking of equipment, sounds I recognized as soldiers marching. But when I looked around there was no one there."

A subsequent trip to Gettysburg proved harrowing for the couple. They decided to stay at the Cashtown Inn, an establishment that has been hosting travelers since the late 18th century. During the battle of Gettysburg the inn served as headquarters for Confederate General A.P. Hill.

"As soon as we got to the inn, I knew something wasn't right," Carole said.

"Like what?" I asked.

"It was just a feeling," she said. "I felt the presence of other people in the place even though there wasn't anyone else there."

"Had you ever felt that before?" I said.

"All my life. I've always had the ability to sense other people around me."

"So, what happened?"

"We were given the A.P. Hill room. That night as we were in bed, I felt something come up on the bed, almost like a cat, but there was no cat. I could feel it moving on the bed. Suddenly, something grabbed my arm and held it hard. I started screaming and woke up Dale. He jumped out of bed and turned on the lights but there was no one in the room besides us."

"And Dale didn't hear or feel anything?" I asked.

"No. I looked at my arm and I had red marks where I had been grabbed. Dale thought maybe he had rolled over in his sleep on my arm, but there was no way that could have happened the way we were positioned."

"What do you think it was?"

"I don't know," Carole said. "I never saw anything. I do know the inn is supposed to be haunted. That's all I can say."

There are some personal ghost stories I trust more than others—I'll admit that, just as there are some story-tellers I trust more than others. Nuns, for example. Judges. Librarians. Okay, I don't know why I trust librarians exactly, but it just seems that I should. Carole is the director of the library in Carver, Massachusetts. I trust her story.

Delicia Wallnofer also had an encounter at the rocky summit known as Little Round Top. It was during her 1998 visit to Gettysburg.

"My two aunts, my grandmother, and my uncle and I had gone up right about sunset and had taken a few pictures with a gentleman who was portraying General Lee," she said. "We decided to walk down the path that Hood's men had advanced. We got to the big rocks and were trying to figure out how we were going to get down them, when a young gentleman, whose uniform I had admired on the way up, told us good evening, complimented us on our looks, and offered to hand us down the rocks so we didn't fall. After he passed us down, we turned around to see my uncle coming down the rocks, but no soldier. We asked a few people around where he had gone, to have them reply that the only person they had seen near us was my uncle."

Apparently, Southern etiquette survives the grave.

Susan Carpenter is a member of the Soldiers' Benevolent Society, civilian reenactors associated with the 26th Regiment North Carolina Troops. During a visit to Gettysburg, she and a few others from her group decided to walk the path taken by troops under Confederate Major General George Pickett as they charged Union positions along Cemetery Ridge. The group started at the stone wall upon the ridge, at the point known as the High Water Mark, and walked the path back to where the ill-fated charge had begun.

"As soon as I stepped out on the path," Susan said, "I could feel the cold coming up from the ground. I began to feel my neck starting to prickle, and my feet and legs were cold. Then I began to hear the moaning and smell the blood, and when I looked down there was no-where to step because there were dead and dying men everywhere. It was really real, but I just kept on walking and saying, 'I am sorry, I am so sorry' in my head. When we got to the other side and turned to go back, suddenly they were gone, the ground was clear, and no one was lying there. But walking back across I could feel them breathing behind me. It was very strange."

There are, of course, many ghostly stories from other Civil War battlefields as well.

In 1995, Jim Mohring from Manly's Battery, 1st North Carolina Battery A, an artillery reenactment group, was at the reenactment celebrating the 130th anniversary of the battle of Saylor's Creek in Virginia. In that engagement large numbers of Confederate troops and several prominent officers surrendered to Union troops, eventually leading up to Robert E. Lee's surrender at Appomattox Courthouse only a few days later.

"A friend and I were talking in front of his tent around 11 p.m. that Friday night," Jim said, "when I caught him gazing down the rather long company street. When I looked in that direction, I saw a Confederate cavalryman, leading his mount up the street; rather inconsiderate of him,

I thought at the time. He looked dead tired, like this was the end of a long, hard day. His head drooped, shoulders slumped, the reins of the horse only half held in his left hand. His clothes were soiled and thin. They were not new wools. I must admit, his impression was the best I had seen, even up to now."

Jim said that the soldier led his horse up the street without saying a word or responding to other reenactors who called out to him as he passed. The next morning Jim stepped out of his tent and, feeling the ground give softly beneath his feet, thought he would be able to follow the horse's trail to see from where the cavalryman had come.

"I started looking," Jim said. "Not a sign. No footprints, no hoof-prints, nothing. I started down the street to where my 16-year-old son had camped campaign style with other boys his age at the end of the street. Next to briars so thick a rabbit couldn't go through. As I walked, I looked at the tents, neatly aligned peg-to-peg right up to the briars. There was no way the cavalryman and his horse could enter the street without leaving some evidence.

"I asked the boys what time they went to sleep and if they had seen anything last night. They said they went to sleep around 1 a.m. and saw or heard nothing. Did I see a ghost? There must be some logical explanation, although, to this day, it has not occurred to me."

The 1862 Battle of Shiloh was one of the bloodiest of the Civil War, with approximately 24,000 killed, wounded, and missing. Shiloh National Military Park today preserves thousands of acres of that contested ground—and may preserve the brave spirits of long-gone soldiers as well.

A Texas reenactor by the name of Hawk* visited Shiloh with a friend. He joined a memorial service of 15 to 20 people gathered around a monument at the park. Hawk removed his hat in honor of the dead and began thinking about the terrible sacrifice the soldiers of 1862 had made.

"I suddenly began to sob uncontrollably," Hawk said. "Not wanting to be embarrassed, I tried to conceal it, but my throat tightened up, and breathing became difficult. Quick, deep gasps. It was embarrassing and a little frightening, since it happened suddenly and surprised me. I am not normally an emotional person. I started to walk away quickly, and then noticed, lying all over the ground in grotesque positions, hundreds of bloody and ragged bodies. They were so many of them, and so close together it was difficult to walk without stepping on them. They were so clearly distinguishable that I was afraid to actually step on them. I detoured around the area where they were mostly concentrated, and walked back to the truck."

Hawk said that he was not one of those reenactors who seek "special moments" at reenactments, but he knew what he had seen at Shiloh and he believed it, even if he couldn't explain it.

Do ghosts really march again at these battlefields? It's difficult to say. Certainly, there are many sane, reasonable people who will swear to having had contact with the paranormal at the places, and I do not doubt their sincere belief in those experiences. But are they witnessing ghosts—once living persons who have lost their way to a better place after death—or are they unwittingly creating the ghosts in their own minds?

I was 10 years old the first time I visited the Gettysburg battlefield, but even at that young age, the place left an indelible impression upon me. Yes, I suppose I was something of a history nerd. Still, the memory of those green rolling fields and rocky ridges, the stonewalls, the solemn monuments standing sentinel throughout the field, and the marble grave markers laid out neatly in the cemetery dedicated by Abraham Lincoln lingers with me today. I didn't see any ghosts, but I could easily understand how a person more sensitive than myself to psychic phenomena could see them, or could think they saw them.

I wish I could tell you definitively whether or not ghosts roam these hallowed battlefields. My guess is that they do, because the memories of those brave men and the sacrifices they made will always be fresh in our minds.

CHAPTER 17

THE ORIGINAL GHOSTHUNTERS

Ed and Lorraine Warren are to ghosthunters what Ben and Jerry are to ice cream lovers. For almost half a century the Warrens have been stars in the world of the paranormal, both here and abroad. In those years, they have investigated more than five thousand cases and have participated in countless "ghostbustings" and exorcisms.

I first met the Warrens in 1993, while I was doing research about Dudleytown, an old ghost town buried in the woods of northwestern Connecticut. I had been traipsing around on the mountaintop where the ruins of Dudleytown were located with Jay Baca, who was something of a local historian and storyteller. We poked through old cellar holes and stone foundations, overgrown with shrubs and weeds. There wasn't anything in particular we were searching for, but we did turn up a broken Ouija board and the stubs of some burned-out candles, unsettling evidence of some occult activity going on there.

We were alone, our footsteps the only sounds in the eerily silent woods. Not so much as a single birdcall. Sunlight filtered through the dense forest canopy only in fits and starts, casting a funereal pall over the site. In days gone by, Dudleytown was nicknamed Dark Entry by the villagers who lived in the valley below, and remnants of the abandoned Dark Entry Road can still be found beneath the oaks and pines. The villagers in the valley used to instill good behavior in their children by telling them that if they were not good, they would bring them up the mountain to the Dudleytown bogeymen; it was that kind of place.

Ed and Lorraine Warren had lived all their lives in Connecticut, and knew the state and its many ghostly residents intimately. By the time I contacted them in 1993, their reputations as ghosthunters and psychic investigators had long been established. They had several books in print and were themselves the subject of many others; were in high demand on the TV, radio, and lecture circuit; and continued to investigate paranormal events all around the world. They had been involved with several well-publicized cases, the most notable being the haunted house in Amityville, New York, in which 23-year-old Ronald DeFeo shot to death his parents and four siblings in 1974. The case later became the subject of the novel and subsequent film, *The Amityville Horror*. The Warrens were two of only a very few psychic investigators allowed on the premises, and they have the only photographs ever taken inside the house. Ed and Lorraine were obvious choices to help me with my research.

I spoke to Lorraine on the phone, introducing myself and telling her about my project. She was gracious and polite, sprinkling her conversation with "dears" just as my grandmother would have, and invited me to visit her and Ed at their home.

The Warrens lived in a small town in Connecticut, a town I also lived in for a few years, although I did not know them at the time I was a resident. On a warm, sunny day in June, following Lorraine's directions, I drove past a reservoir with dead trees standing in black water with bright green lily pads floating on the impenetrable surface, and turned onto a small dead-end road surrounded by deep woods. Only a few houses stood on the road. The Warren house, a nondescript one-level house nestled beneath tall trees, was at the end of the road. The dense woods, owned and preserved by the local water utility as a watershed for the reservoir, came right up to their property. At night, owls hooted in the branches above their roof.

I parked my car in front of the house and got out. Cicadas buzzed in the hot air. Shafts of sunlight shot through the trees. I saw that the front door of the house was open, leaving only the screen door closed. I walked up to the door and rang the bell. I waited. No one came to the door. I rang the bell again. Nothing. I peered through the screen into the gloom inside the house.

"Hello?" I called through the screen.

A little yappy dog came out of nowhere, throwing itself against the screen, barking its fool head off at me. I jumped back, startled by its sudden appearance. I was sure the barking dog would get the Warrens' attention, but no one came.

The driveway sloped down to the rear of the house and I decided to walk down it, thinking maybe the Warrens were outside in the back. A chain-link fence flanked the drive and enclosed the rear yard. My attention was drawn to an addition to the house, a barn-like annex with several windows. Through the glass I saw strange and horrible masks hanging on the walls. Protruding tongues, bulging eyes, horns. I would have studied these weird objects more closely had not another dog, this time a lunatic German Shepard, leapt at the chain-link fence, threatening to dismember me if he got through. I beat it out of there.

I didn't think either dog could chew its way through metal, but I wasn't positively sure, so I sat in my car waiting for the Warrens. Only a few minutes later, a car turned into the driveway, and Ed and Lorraine got out. They were older than I had expected, maybe in their 60s. Ed was a big man, solid, with close-cropped hair, and a slight smile that seemed to hide secrets. He could have been a bouncer in a bar, except that he was friendly...so maybe a friendly bouncer.

Lorraine, on the other hand, was tall and thin, with the misleading fragile looks of a porcelain doll. She was dressed conservatively but fashionably in a long skirt and blazer, her salt-and-pepper hair pulled back in a bun, tied with a scarf. She was recovering from an auto accident and walked with the assistance of a metal walker.

Ed and Lorraine Warren.
Courtesy of Lorraine Warren.

As we stood on the front porch, they apologized for being late. I said I hadn't been there all that long, but I remarked that I was surprised they had gone out and left the house open. Didn't they worry about someone getting inside? Robbing them?

Lorraine looked at me and said, without a trace of humor, "Who would ever break into our house?"

I thought of the dogs, but mostly of the weird masks in the back, and thought she was probably right. You'd have to be crazy, or carrying some serious juju, to break into the house of the Warrens.

We all went inside. I didn't know if it was the lack of many windows or just the deep shade cast by the surrounding woods that made the interior so dark. Cool enough in the heat, that was true, but gloomy just the same. The house was a museum to their lives. Every bit of wall space was covered. Paintings, photos, ceramic plates, tapestries, and various art objects, planters, sconces—anything and everything that could be fastened to a wall had found a place here. As if that wasn't bad enough, this vertical treasure trove went horizontal as well, spilling over onto every available surface: more framed photos, religious statues, figurines of various sorts, coasters, travel keepsakes. This house had it all.

It seemed to me that most of the objects decorating their house were of a religious nature, which came as no surprise, because the Warrens were devout Catholics and frequently thought of their life's work in terms of good against evil, God against Satan. In fact, before the notorious Amityville case made them nationally famous, the Warrens had gone about their work in an almost invisible manner, well known to various clergymen who consulted them on cases of demonic possession, but otherwise unknown to the general public.

Very few people grow up with the intention of becoming professional ghosthunters, and the Warrens were no exception, although it did seem that fate was pushing them in that direction. Married just after Ed's World War II tour of duty in the military, the young couple decided to become landscape artists, as both had had some schooling in the arts. They traveled around New England and other locations, scouting out appropriate models for their paintings, invariably being drawn to old, run-down, or abandoned houses. As they painted, they would talk to the people who lived in the houses or were neighbors to them and learned what they could about the history of each of them. Lorraine made an interesting discovery of her own as they traveled to these places: Her natural clairvoyant abilities, which she had tried to suppress as a teenager, were now coming forward, perhaps tweaked by the psychic emanations from the old houses. Ghosts and haunted houses were nothing new for Ed; at the age of 5 he had seen the dead landlady of the building he lived in materialize before his very eyes, and had often had prophetic dreams of a nun who came to talk with him. Ed described the woman to his father, who recognized her as his own sister. This aunt had died before Ed was born.

We sat in the parlor and I proceeded to tell the Warrens about my visit to Dudleytown. I told them about finding a broken Ouija board in an old cellar hole.

"I'm not at all surprised that you found a board there," Ed said, shaking his head. "That place is truly haunted. If people only knew, a Ouija board is not a toy. It's a means of communicating with the spirit world. It open doors for spirits to enter, but you never know what kind of spirit will come through."

"We've almost never seen a positive spirit communicate through a Ouija board," Lorraine added.

"Here, look at these," Ed said, handing me several color photos. "I dug these out of the files for you to see."

Ed leaned forward on the sofa as I looked through the photos. Every now and then he would point out some detail to make sure I didn't miss anything. The photos showed Ed and Lorraine and a few other people at Dudleytown. In several of the photos swirling mists or streaks were visible. Sometimes floating orbs of light were caught in the photos.

"All of those things indicate the presence of spirits," Lorraine said. "They need energy to materialize and they were drawn to the energy that came from the auras of our group."

I certainly hadn't seen any of those things when I had been at Dudleytown, but then Lorraine explained to me that the mysterious shapes and lights had not been visible to any of them at the time either; they only showed up on the film after it had been developed. I, too, had taken some photos while I was at Dudleytown, but had not yet had them developed.

Ed was holding the last photo. "This one is very odd," he said, handing it to me. There were two or three people in the photo, a dense stand of trees behind them. In the lower right corner was a small blurry object that looked similar to a hot dog wearing a red knit cap.

"What is it?" I asked.

Ed shrugged. "I'm not entirely sure, but it's not human, that much I can tell you."

I thought it looked as if someone had gotten a thumb in front of the lens, but I didn't say anything. Ed had been at this sort of thing a lot longer than me. Strangely enough, when I finally did get my pictures back from the photo lab it appeared that I had captured the image of a leathery face at the edge of a cellar hole. I would have been reluctant to swear in a court of law that it really was a face, but it sure looked to be one. We talked for a while, Ed and Lorraine graciously sharing with me all that they knew about Dudleytown, and then I left.

Fast forward 11 years to 2004, and I was once again on the phone with Lorraine Warren, this time inviting her to be a part of this book. We agreed to meet on one of my trips back to Connecticut when I was visiting with some of my family. It was once again a warm, sunny day in June as I pulled up in front of the house. Everything looked to my eye as it did 11 years before. But there had been some big changes.

Several years after my visit to the Warrens, Ed had suffered a massive stroke, and now the man I remembered as hale and hearty and energetic, sat slumped in a wheelchair decorated with a Mylar smiley-face balloon, his paralyzed legs bowed, feet crossed at the ankles, his arms lying uselessly in his lap, his head lolling to one side. Unable to speak, he could only emit involuntary howls and groans. I was stunned by the change in the man I once knew, but Lorraine fussed over him and spoke to him as she had always done, his awful debilitation invisible to her loving eyes.

A little later, after Lorraine got Ed settled in the house with an aide she had hired, we were sitting in a restaurant in nearby Newtown, talking. I didn't want to dwell on anything painful for Lorraine, but I couldn't help but wonder how Ed's condition affected their work and how difficult it must be for her to take care of him.

"Taking care of Ed," Lorraine said. "You don't know how that is. You don't know, John, how blessed I feel to be able to have God entrust such a special guy to me. I never think for one minute that this is a burden. Oh no, honey, believe me, it's not."

I believed her. After all, this is the same woman who, as a teenager, after meeting Ed for the first time, wrote in her diary, I will spend the rest of my life with you. Fully 59 years later she was doing just that.

As I sat across the table from Lorraine, I marveled at how little she had changed in the 11 years since I had last seen her. Thin as ever, stylish but conservatively dressed as always, her hair a bit grayer but still fashioned in her trademark bun adorned with a scarf, she exuded enthusiasm and energy that I rarely see in people half her age.

Even with Ed sidelined by his medical condition, Lorraine kept up the work the two had started so long ago. She continues on the college lecture circuit, now assisted by her son-in-law; she has filmed a promotional trailer for the remake of *The Amityville Horror*; she was in negotiations with various TV and film producers about creating paranormal programs and movies; she was finishing up a new book, *Ghost Tracks*; and she was still actively working as a paranormal investigator.

"I don't sit around knitting, dear," Lorraine said. "As soon as you slow down, you get rusty."

"Tell me about some of the investigations you're doing now," I said.

"I got a call from a woman who is a paralegal. She said they see this shadowy black figure, no face. This thing has been witnessed by every member of the family. They see it go down the hallway. It will come into the room. It's been going on for a period of time. It goes away and comes back again. She just wanted to have the knowledge of what was going on and why. I said, What is your religion?

Catholic.

I said, You're not practicing are you?

No.

How old are your children?

Sixteen and 20.

I said, Is there turmoil in your house?

Yeah, a lot. What part does that play?

I said, It's breaking down the structure of your family. Is your husband still living in that home?

No.

Everything was there, John. They can't see the fire for the smoke."

"What did you do?" I asked.

"I said to the woman, Let's start with your daughter, who I believe is the catalyst. Let's start by having her baptismal vows renewed.

She doesn't believe in God anymore.

They can't see it, John, they cannot see it," Lorraine said, slapping her hand on the table for emphasis. "Anyway, I went on and told her what we would be able to do. She said she'd have to talk it over with her family. I asked her if she really believed she was going to get the cooperation of her son and her daughter, when they didn't believe in one solitary thing I was talking about. I gave her my home phone number and told her she could contact me anytime. I have to just wait now."

"So which comes first?" I asked Lorraine. "Is it a bad family situation that causes the haunting, or is it the other way around, or both?"

"It's both, honey. I asked that woman when the thing comes back if there is a lot of turmoil in the house at that time, a lot of fighting, and she says, Oh, yes. It's hard to keep peace in this house. I said, How can you keep peace in a house that's void of anything spiritual? So, I'll wait for now, I'll wait and see what happens. If she calls, it would be wonderful."

Our waiter came over to ask us if everything was to our satisfaction. We told him everything was fine and then Lorraine told him that he resembled Ronald Reagan's son. She couldn't remember the son's name and neither could I. The young waiter probably didn't know who Ronald Reagan was, let alone his son. He seemed perplexed, but smiled politely anyway.

"You really do, honey," Lorraine said, as he collected the remains of our lunch.

"Why did you ask the woman to have her daughter renew her baptismal vows?" I asked.

"It's important to get your baptismal vows renewed because these vows are a form of exorcism," Lorraine said. "Every Easter vigil every Catholic can do it because that's what they do in a Catholic church at that time. I can't tell you how many people I've told that to. I love to do it. I like the idea of voluntarily being able to do it."

"I know for you and Ed, your work has always been about spirituality," I said.

"Oh my, yes," she said. "Ed would never admit to being psychic but probably nobody in this country, or out of this country, is as knowledgeable as him in the field of religious demonology. He was called by clergy all over the world, be they Mormons, be they Buddhists, be they Anglicans, be they Hebrews, it didn't matter. In the weeks just before he collapsed we were in the mountains of Japan working with Buddhist monks. Oh, yes."

She was quiet for a few moments, eyes fixed on some point behind me, and I knew she was lost in some memory of the past.

"You know, dear," she finally said, "Ed and I look back on our lives since we became public figures in 1969 and say, 'Was that really us that all this happened to?'" She shook her head slowly, as if she couldn't believe her own memories. "I was brought up in a very loving, secure Irish Catholic home. There was no talk of stuff like that," she said, referring to her psychic abilities. "As long as it was like a parlor game I wouldn't be serious about it, so I suppressed it. But we became artists, making our living as artists, and as we went into these old houses to satisfy Ed's curiosity, my psychic ability started to develop naturally."

"And as a result you've been able to help many people."

"Oh, yes. Even with Ed's collapse God is allowing me to help these people without jeopardizing my time with my husband. We've always had faith. I don't believe my husband would be here without prayer. Everything is based on faith, dear."

***

Postscript: In 2006, as I was completing this book, Ed Warren finally succumbed to his illness. He will be sorely missed.

Chapter 18

Holy Ghosts

When I was a child I was taught to bless myself before saying prayers with the words, In the name of the Father, and of the Son, and of the Holy Ghost. I understood the words father and son easily enough, although I may not have gotten the full religious implications of those words, but what exactly was a holy ghost? The good sisters who taught my catechism class never spoke about ghosts, nor did the Holy Cross fathers who taught at my high school. Even in the Catholic university I attended, there was no mention of ghosts, although by then the word spirit was being used more often than ghost. It seemed odd that ghosts and spirits would be mentioned in prayers, yet they never figured more prominently than that in my religious instruction.

Perhaps that confusion about ghosts and spirits is what led me to inquire about the Spiritualist Church. After all, Spiritualists believe not only that there is another existence after this earthly life, as do many other religions, but that the dead, those who are now "in spirit," as the Spiritualists say, are still very much with the living. Unlike most other religions that believe in an afterlife in which the dead are shunted off to some spiritual abode clearly separate from the living, Spiritualists do not believe those two worlds are separated at all. The dead actually coexist with the living in a spiritual world that overlaps the material world. In fact, it is possible for those who have died to communicate with the living through mediums and psychics, to offer the living comfort, support, and advice. Communicating with spirits is the heart of the Spiritualist Church.

At the invitation of Reverend Rose Vanden Eynden, I attended a service at United Spiritualists of the Christ Light church in Blue Ash, Ohio. The church itself was located in a nondescript brick building in a business park, and I wasn't certain I was in the right place until I noticed a silver SUV in the parking lot with a license plate that read "SPIRTED."

Rose pulled into the parking lot almost simultaneously. I got out of my car and closed the door, locking the keys inside. No spare key, of course. That didn't bode well, I thought, but Rose was waiting for me; I'd have to deal with the problem later. She greeted me with a hug and escorted me into the building.

The church occupied a suite of rooms on the second floor. People were milling about in the small reception area and each of them welcomed me warmly to the service. There was a desk in the room and a bulletin board, below which a table held an assortment of brochures and pamphlets about Spiritualism and information about church activities.

I was surprised to see a few children at the service, somehow thinking that Spiritualism was for adults. There was a room behind the reception area specifically set up for children's bible study, stocked with books, games, and arts and crafts supplies. It all seemed cheery and bright, despite the fact that the children's instructor was a guy who wore a Van Helsing overcoat. Still, he seemed nice enough.

Down the hall there were a few more small offices for the ministers and staff, and beyond that was the worship space, a large room with rows of maroon chairs, comfortably upholstered—so much better than the bone-jarring wooden pews I knew—and a single window that ran the entire length of one wall.

Rose was attending to some church business, so I seated myself in one of the chairs, waiting for the service to begin. I had never been inside a Spiritualist church before and had no idea what to expect. I was surprised to find how familiar the surroundings seemed to me. A simple wooden lectern stood at the front of the room. Behind it, against the wall, was a small table with a floral arrangement upon it. The table was flanked by two candle stands, each holding a single tall candle. A portrait of Jesus hung above the table. Half a dozen or so chairs were set off to one side for the choir. The choirmaster, dressed in a black gown, was already softly playing a hymn on an electronic keyboard.

The minister entered wearing a black gown and a white stole embroidered with an eagle and we were off and running. The service was very similar to what I knew from my own Catholic background: a choir singing hymns, an exchange of peace greetings among the congregation, the Lord's Prayer, an offertory collection, and a sensible sermon about the power of words to hurt or heal that could have been delivered in any church anywhere. I did notice that references to God were usually stated as Mother-Father God, a term that would not fly in the patriarchal Catholic Church, but all the other outward signs and symbols of worship seemed traditionally Christian.

The service lasted about 45 minutes, followed by church announcements. Then the minister stood and said, "Now for the part of our service that makes us unique." He introduced Lucinda*, a middle-aged woman who was studying to become a medium. She wore a fancy black dress and had her blond hair swept up and styled. This was her first time "on the platform," meaning the first time she was giving a public spirit reading.

Lucinda began by telling the audience who were the spirits there to help her with her reading. She held her arms out to her sides, continually rubbing her thumb and fingers together as if she were generating electricity. She paced back and forth before the audience, rubbing her fingers, concentrating, before delivering some of the images she was receiving from spirits. She talked about being shown a waterfall, and a woman in the audience said that image pertained to her. Lucinda walked closer to the woman and told her that the spirits were saying the waterfall meant the woman would be invigorated, would receive new energy in her life and that she should accept that energy and not fear it. The woman smiled, nodded her head, and said, "Bless you."

"Bless you," Lucinda replied.

She received the image of a seed, with which a man in the congregation identified, and Lucinda told him it meant that he was "putting down deep roots and was growing."

While Lucinda was working with the audience, the minister sat in a chair off to one side, watching her, studying her movements, and listening carefully to her words. He was clearly judging her work, using criteria completely unknown to me.

Frankly, I thought these spirit messages were pretty vague, but then I remembered Lucinda was only a student medium and that this was her first time giving a reading. What more could I expect? After a few more minutes the minister allowed her to take her seat. It seemed that both he and the audience were satisfied with Lucinda's debut.

A spry, energetic woman with a single long braid trailing down her back followed Lucinda. She was an ordained minister, a certified medium, and an old hand at spirit readings. She bounced around the front of the room, quickly calling out names and images. Several people in the audience responded to her, sometimes in tears, happy to have received a communication from a departed loved one. After each message there was the exchange of "Bless you."

"I'm getting a Harry," she said, at one point. "Who has a Harry?" Several hands shot up, but she went over to a woman a few rows from the front and said, "Spirit is leading me to you. Harry. A family member?"

Reverend Rose Vanden Eynden.
Courtesy of John Kachuba.

"Yes," the woman said. "Actually, Harriet, but we called her Harry."
The medium nodded. "Yes, your maternal grandmother, right?"
"Yes, that's right."

The medium then gave her a message that made no sense to me, but had the woman nodding her head enthusiastically, tears brimming in her eyes. "Bless you," she murmured.

The reading went on for another 20 minutes before the service was finally concluded. No spirit contacted me. Afterwards, I sat down with Rose Vanden Eynden in her office to ask her some questions about Spiritualism. I was still confused by the notion of Christian Spiritualists and asked Rose to explain that for me.

Rose said that she was raised as a Catholic, but that she later became interested in Wicca, and then Spiritualism. She said that the United Spiritualists of the Christ Light church, which she helped found, called itself a Christian church by choice because so many church members had originally been brought up in Christian denominations and still held an affinity for the Bible and the teachings of Jesus. She said that most Spiritualist churches would not refer to themselves as Christian.

"There are usually three kinds of Spiritualist churches," Rose said. "There are those that are true to the Spiritualist way of looking at things, which is that everything is inclusive. Most of the time, when these churches talk about God, they talk about God as an infinite intelligence, rather than a creator or God with male connotations. They tend to look at things from broader perspective. Then there are Christian Spiritualist churches which tend to look at things from a Christian standpoint, and then lastly, there is sort of an eastern philosophy of Spiritualism."

"But the portrait of Jesus was front and center in your services," I said.

"Yes, although we don't believe that Jesus is God in the respect that most Christian denominations believe in Jesus as God. We believe that we are all God and that Jesus as Christ was the Christ here on this Earth, [then] became the Christ, and so we all have that ability to come to that level of Christ-ness. We don't even look at him as Son of God the way that most Christian denominations do. Sometimes we get into splitting hairs over that too because we have some in our population who don't even like it that we use the word Lord, or those kinds of things, and then we have those who do like those things and think of Jesus in a higher entity sort of way."

"So, what then are the basic principles of Spiritualism?"

"All Spiritualist churches have nine principles," Rose said, "although our church has added some to the original nine and we now have 16. The most important principles are, that in spiritualism we believe in God, some force that oversees things. We believe that everybody is responsible for his own actions, and we do not believe in vicarious atonement, which means that anyone can take away someone else's sins. The idea of Jesus as savior doesn't fly in the Spiritualist Church; that idea is a huge separation from other Christian denominations. We also believe, of course, in after-death communication and the idea that we can communicate with spirits.

"After-death communication is for most people what Spiritualism is really about," Rose said. "It's about contacting their dead folks and knowing that there is life after death and that there is something beyond this body and that we go on from here into another place and that we continue to exist, we continue to learn.

"For me, that's a really important component of after-death communication, helping people to realize that Mom is dead, yes, but she's alive on the other side, and on the other side she's becoming even closer to who she's supposed to be because she's continuing on, she's continuing to grow, even if we don't see that every time when she comes through. I lost my mom five years ago and I love to hear from her. When my mom comes through, it's always a blessing."

"I don't understand what you mean when you say she's closer to 'who she's supposed to be.' Can you explain that?" I asked.

"When you have a relationship with your spirit guides and you have a relationship with speaking to spirit, then you also have this ability, I think, to see a bigger picture and to see a clearer picture of where your life is probably going to go," Rose said. "For me, that's a huge blessing because so many of us are stumbling around in the dark a lot. Speaking with spirit gives you a clearer idea of where your life should be going. I believe that we come into this world with certain things that we're supposed to be doing, that we've made a contract, so to speak, to do something, but we've forgotten that in our humanness, when we come into our human bodies. So, to be able to meditate on that and have a communication with those in spirit who can help us remember those things a little better is very helpful."

I had noticed during the service that most of the audience members were female, which reminded me of the other Spiritualist ministers I had met over the past year, all of whom were women. This was a striking difference to the church in which I was raised where women are relegated to second-class citizenship. I asked Rose why women were so prevalent among Spiritualists. She agreed that Spiritualism offered women leadership roles that would be denied them in many other patriarchal faiths, and also thought the lack of hierarchy in Spiritualist churches was appealing to women, again because they would not be restricted from reaching their full potential for participation in the church. Rose also thought the Spiritualist Church offered an inclusive philosophy that women found attractive.

"I think there is a female side to God, which was something we didn't talk about in the Catholic Church," Rose said. "There was Mary, but she wasn't on the same level with everybody else. I believe the creator is both male and female, if you can even define creator in those terms. There's got to be balance in the universe, so there's got to be masculine and feminine."

It's no surprise, really, that Spiritualists are predominantly women, because modern-day Spiritualism was made popular by Catherine and Margaretta Fox, sisters who first began hearing unexplainable knocking and rapping sounds in their Hydesville, New York, home in 1848. The girls developed a system of communication with the entity, which they determined to be the spirit of Charles B. Rosna, who had been purportedly murdered by the previous owner of the house. Prodded by their older sister, Mrs. Leah Fish, the young girls were soon on tour demonstrating their ability to talk with the dead, promoted for part of the time by the great showman P.T. Barnum. Spiritualism, the belief in communication with the dead, was soon flourishing throughout the country, with the first church established in 1853. During the bloody carnage of the Civil War, Spiritualist practices comforted thousands of grieving people, including Mary Todd Lincoln, who held séances to commune both with her deceased sons and, later, her murdered husband.

Embedded with the Paranormal Paramilitary
Riding with Mediums, Spirit Seekers, and Ghost Hunters
194

The religion quickly spread to the United Kingdom, where it enjoyed great popularity, especially during World War I. Among its adherents abroad were such notables as Sir Arthur Conan Doyle, whose son was killed in the war, and Queen Victoria.

Although most of the practitioners of Spiritualism were sincere in their beliefs, there were also a number of notorious charlatans who were

Colby Memorial Temple at Cassadaga, Florida.
Courtesy of John Kachuba.

eventually unmasked by the magician Harry Houdini and other investigators. These fakes caused irreparable harm to the Spiritualists, and the popularity of the church declined.

There has recently been renewed interest in the beliefs of Spiritualism as evidenced by the popularity of mediums such as Sylvia Browne and John Edward, and television programs such as *Medium* and *Ghost Whisperer*, but that interest has not brought the religion of Spiritualism back to the level of popularity it once held. It remains a small religion of loosely organized churches scattered across the country, with some Spiritualist "camps" maintaining the old ways and preserving the spirit of Spiritualism. Two of the most famous of these camps are Lily Dale in upper New York state and Cassadaga in Florida.

When still a young man, New Yorker George Colby was told during a séance that he would one day be instrumental in establishing a Spiritualist community in the South. Following the instructions of Seneca, his Indian spirit guide, Colby headed south in 1875 and settled in central Florida. Here, he homesteaded land, and in 1895 deeded 35 acres to the newly incorporated Cassadaga Spiritualist Camp Meeting Association. Today, the community comprises about 57 acres and has 55 residences. It is home to like-minded people who share Spiritualist beliefs. About 25 of these residents are mediums who offer consultations in their homes.

A glance at the map I had obtained at the rental car counter showed me that tiny Cassadaga was located midway between Daytona and Orlando. It was 9 a.m. on a weekday when I turned off County Road 4139 at the Cassadaga sign and parked in a little gravel lot beside the bookstore and visitor center.

I stepped up onto the verandah. A large sign mounted on the wall proudly proclaimed that I had indeed arrived at the Southern Cassadaga Spiritualist Camp Meeting Association. The sign listed the schedule of worship and healing services and invited visitors to "inquire here for readings from 40 certified mediums, healing center hours, and all camp activities," which I presumed did not mean archery or volleyball. The door was locked; the store didn't open until 10 a.m. With an hour to kill I decided to see the town.

I walked down Stevens Street, a narrow paved road flanked on both sides by dwellings that displayed a mix of architectural styles, mostly wood-frame houses, ranging from "Florida cracker" bungalows and cottages to larger, two-story, Queen Anne–style homes enclosed by picket fences. The homes were nestled beneath tall trees and surrounded by lush shrubbery and flowering plants, giving the place the look and feel of an old summer resort, which was, in fact, what it had once been for rich Spiritualist snowbirds in the Victorian era.

A few other streets branched off Stevens from the right and worked their way up the hills. That's right: hills in Florida. Maybe not the kind

Spirit Pond at Cassadaga, Florida.
Courtesy of John Kachuba.

of hills I knew growing up in New England, but for Florida, these were the Rockies. Little parks with benches and flowery plantings were scattered throughout the town and bore names such as Medicine Wheel, Black Hawk, and Seneca, commemorating both George Colby's spirit guide, Seneca, and the affinity Spiritualists seem to have for Native Americans. Apparently, everyone has a Native American spirit guide, which means that either there were once many more Native Americans in this country than we thought, or that they are earning some serious overtime pay in the afterlife.

I was struck by the complete and utter silence of the town. No voices, no cars, not even bird song. It was as though nature conspired with the Spiritualists to make the place as still and contemplative as possible. Perhaps Colby had truly been led there by his spirit guide for exactly that reason. Other than a fat gray cat slinking across the road, I saw no signs of life.

At Seneca Park, a large expanse of grass and trees sloped down to Spirit Pond. I sat on a stone bench, drinking in the mysterious ambience of the town. A large house sat across the pond, partly concealed in the fringe of trees circling the water. A few puffy clouds swam by overhead, mirrored in the tranquil pond. I could smell the earth where I sat, a deep, loamy scent, touched with a hint of something floral. Jasmine? The bench was placed at the foot of a large tree and I peered up through the branches, looking for birds. No birds. But I did spy a green wire meticulously fashioned into a noose hanging from one of the branches. That got me up and walking again.

I walked back up Stevens Street, past the two-story Harmony Hall where many of the mediums hung out their shingles—in a sort of medium shopping mall—and settled myself on the verandah of the cream-colored Cassadaga Hotel, located across the street from the bookstore. The verandah was a large one, and several tables and chairs were arranged along its length, but I was the only person there. I went over to the lobby door, found it locked, and looked in through the glass. Not a soul.

Just as I was wondering if perhaps the Spiritualists were here in spirit only, I heard music. Loud music. An old white Mercury, the size of an amphibious assault vehicle, cruised past the hotel. An equally large man dressed in a colorful Hawaiian style shirt was jammed behind the wheel, a straw planter's hat pulled down to his sunglasses. All the windows in the car were rolled down and—I swear this really happened—the lyrics of a Ruben Studdard song blared out: "I need an angel. I'm calling an angel. Send me an angel. Send an angel down right now. Send an angel down right now." The car passed by and it was quiet once more.

Across the street I noticed activity within the bookstore and saw a woman come out, unlock the door, and go back inside. I waited just a few minutes before going over. I inquired about mediums and she directed me to an area of the store where mediums had pinned their business cards to a bulletin board. An erasable board listed the names of the mediums that were available that day. A telephone sat on a small cloth-draped table near the board. I scanned the business cards and was attracted to the artwork on one, an eagle against a full sun. I read the name on the card, checked it against the list, and found that Vera* was indeed available. Over the phone she told me she could see me in 15 minutes and gave me directions to her house.

I found Vera's house with no trouble and knocked on the side door as she had instructed. The woman who answered the door was about my age, slim, dark-haired, and completely un-mediumistic looking. She invited me into her consultation area, a small room that had once been an enclosed porch. Vera seated herself in a comfortable chair behind a small writing desk while I sat across from her. She poured out a few drops of some kind of oil from a bottle into her hands, worked it into her fingers and brushed them lightly across her face. Something about clarifying, she said.

Vera asked me if I was trying to contact a particular person who was now "in spirit," or if I wanted a general reading. I chose the latter. She asked me a few questions, which I tried to answer as fully as I could without giving her too much information that she could later recite back to me as advice from the spirits. I felt guilty in holding back because I knew this was how mediums operated. Just as a physician asks you questions about your health in order to diagnose and treat you properly, a medium asks questions about your life in order to better understand the impressions she is receiving and how they may relate to your life. Still, I could not turn off my suspicions.

Vera told me that I had been "living out of a suitcase," which was true; I had been traveling a lot as I researched this book. She said I was "tired," which insight did not require a Ph.D. in psychology. She talked about my three children, calling one "optimistic," another "creative, but not yet successful," and the third "a late bloomer." I didn't find these observations to be particularly impressive, either. I also was not impressed by the fact that she answered her cell phone three times during my $50 session to schedule appointments for other clients. Wasn't she supposed to be concentrating on me? Is there such a thing as mediumistic multi-tasking?

Vera called my wife Mary "a driving force," which is true—too true—and she thought that we would do well living in Georgia, Tennessee, or North Carolina. Finally, and most importantly, Vera said that my writing career was "just about there, financially."

My session with Vera more closely resembled chatting with a friend about my life than receiving any great piece of advice I had not yet considered on my own. But, I did like what Vera said about my future financial success. Think about that as you hold this book in your hands. Could it be the spirits led you to this very book in order to help me? If so, I thank those spirits, and of course, I am grateful to you.

Harmony Hall at Cassadaga, Florida.
Courtesy of John Kachuba.

CHAPTER 19

THE REAL GHOST WHISPERER

"Let's face it," said Mary Ann Winkowski. "The only thing the same between me and Jennifer Love Hewitt is that we both have brown eyes."

Mary Ann was more substantially built than Hewitt and had a few years on the actress who stars in CBS's *Ghost Whisperer* as Melinda Gordon, a woman who can see and talk to ghosts, a character inspired by the true-life experiences of Mary Ann. But as she sat in a Bob Evans restaurant in Mansfield, Ohio, talking with me and my wife, Mary, the real-life ghost whisperer was no less vivacious and outgoing, Midwest-warm and friendly, exactly the kind of person with whom a lonesome ghost would want to have a conversation.

Mary Ann Winkowski

Mary Ann Winkowski,
the real Ghost Whisperer.
Courtesy of Mary Ann Winkowski.

For more than half a century Mary Ann has been seeing and talking to dead people, but only before they "cross over," as she says. "What I do is really narrow. Everyone thinks there is so much more that I do, but I don't think so."

"You see and talk to dead people. That's a pretty major thing," I said. "How do you do that?"

"Number one, I'm a paranormal investigator," Mary Ann said. "I'm not a medium, I'm not a psychic. I couldn't tell you what's going to happen tomorrow any more than anyone else. A medium speaks to spirits that have crossed over, not earthbound spirits. I can only see and talk to earthbound spirits. The earthbound spirits are the ones that give you problems, okay? The ones that crossed over are done, they're content, they're where they need to be."

She paused as the waitress brought our lunch order and set it down in front of us. The restaurant was crowded and noisy, and probably no one was paying any attention to the three of us talking, or to the tape recorder placed upon the table, but still I wondered what the other patrons would think if they had overheard our conversation.

Mary Ann continued her thoughts when the waitress left. "People invite me into their homes, okay, and I talk to the spirits and find out who they are and why they didn't cross over. I make the white light and watch them cross over into it and they're where they need to be. It's simple stuff. People try to make it so hard. It's not, it's really easy."

She did make it sound simple, and maybe it was that uncomplicated for her. After all, she'd been doing this since she was 4 years old and her Italian grandmother began taking her to funerals. Her earliest recollection of her special ability came from an incident when she was just a child in Catholic school. She saw the figure of a man close to one of her classmates and told one of the nuns about it. The nun told her it was only the child's guardian angel, but Mary Ann had seen pictures of guardian angels—wings, ruddy cheeks, curly blond hair, blue eyes—and the man she saw didn't look that way. Two weeks later she saw the man beside her classmate while they were on the playground. As before, no one else saw the man except her, and as before, she told a nun about the stranger, only to receive the guardian angel explanation yet again, an explanation she just couldn't accept. When she told her grandmother about the incident, her grandmother immediately recognized that Mary Ann had special abilities and began taking her to the funerals of friends and family members in order to develop her talents for communicating with the dead.

"Did your grandmother have those abilities as well?" Mary asked.

"If you had a ghost in your house," Mary Ann said, "and Grandma slept on your couch, she would get up in the morning and tell you who was there. She couldn't see them when she was awake. Grandma would also get that feeling that someone had died. She would go to sleep and dream about who died. She'd wake up in the morning, go across the street and say, 'Hey, Rose, your brother Luigi died last night,' and sure enough, six or seven weeks later, the letter would come from Italy saying Luigi had died."

"Okay," I said, "but you don't see ghosts in dreams; you see them in real life. How does that work?"

"If I don't make eye contact with them, they don't know I can see them," Mary Ann said. "It's the same when I go to a funeral home, okay? I literally have to walk up to the foot of the casket, look at him, and go, 'Hey, Joe, how are you doing?' I have to pretty much let them know I can see them. These people haven't talked to anybody for a long time, and when they know you can talk to them, it's like somebody drops a quarter in their ear and their mouth just goes," she said, laughing. "I have to try and block it out sometimes. For instance, if I do a public building, like the county morgue, or city hospitals, I can't listen to them all because I'd make myself crazy. It's like, 'You want to go? You want me to make the light? Get in line.'"

The waitress refilled our glasses, and while she did, I looked out the window at the bright December sunlight washing over the snow-patched parking lot, reflecting off Mary Ann's silver Cadillac with its "SPIRIT" license plate. When the waitress moved on to another table, Mary asked Mary Ann to tell us more about what she does at funerals.

Mary Ann explained that she works by a set of rules she has developed over the years. Her cardinal rule is that she has to be invited to the

Embedded with the Paranormal Paramilitary
Riding with Mediums, Spirit Seekers, and Ghost Hunters
204

funeral by an immediate member of the family. No one else can invite her. "You can't believe the nosy neighbors that would call and ask me to come," she said.

The only exception to that rule is in the case of an employer who is attending the funeral of an employee. She will allow the employer to ask only one question of the ghost: What's the password for the work computer? "If they like the boss, the ghosts will give it to them, but if they don't, they'll give them the salute," Mary Ann said, referring to the infamous Italian middle-finger gesture.

"Everyone attends their funeral," Mary Ann said. "Everybody likes to see what their funeral looks like. The ghost is always there. Always. You walk up to a casket to pay your last respects; the dead person's head is to your left, the feet to your right. Standing right there at the foot of the casket is the spirit of whoever died. By standing right there, they can hear everything their family says, they can check out their clothes and what their hair looks like. The women will check out the flowers; the guys—and I don't know if it's a guy thing or what—have to count how many cars are in the funeral procession to the cemetery, the more the better."

She laughed when she said that, her eyes twinkling behind the round frames of her glasses.

"During the service in the cemetery is when most of them just walk into that bright white light," Mary Ann continued. "The very second they took their last breath that white light was right there with them. They actually can see people in that light that they know. They can't talk to them but they're getting this, 'Come on, come on.'

"But you still have free will. If you don't want to go to that light you don't have to go, okay? That light will stay with you for about 72 to 80 hours after the cemetery, which really gives you enough time to go flitting around, be nosy, go to people's houses. No one's going to know you're there, but that light's going to start getting smaller and smaller and if you don't go to it before it disappears, you're stuck."

"Earthbound?"

She nodded her head.

"You don't age when you're earthbound," Mary Ann said. "You don't get taller, smarter, skinnier, nothing. You stay the way you were. By the time I run across these people, they're pretty much willing to go. They've had it. They couldn't evolve. They're stuck in between. That's what I think is so sad."

"Why would someone choose not to go into the light?" I said.

"People don't go for all kinds of reasons: unfinished business, maybe somebody's holding them here, suicides hardly ever cross over, somebody who's been murdered—they're not going to cross over until they find the somebody who took them. A young woman steps off the curb and gets hit by a bus—she's got a 4-year-old and a brand new baby [at] home—you think she's going to leave her kids? Of course not.

"If I died and made the choice not to cross over, I'd be in Paris, I'd be in New York, I'd go anywhere I want, but I couldn't stay in the house. But people do what they're used to doing. People are creatures of habit even when they're dead."

While Mary Ann took a bite of her sandwich, I leaned over and checked the tape recorder. Batteries often go dead when ghosts were around, and even though Mary Ann hadn't said that any ghosts were present in the restaurant, I was taking no chances. The recorder was still working fine.

"You run across a 19-year-old kid who was drunk and wrapped his car around a tree," Mary Ann continued, "and he's standing there at the foot of his casket saying, 'I don't want to be dead, no one's going to tell me where I am going and I'm not going.' He's not going to go, okay? He's going to end up at somebody's house with a bad attitude."

"Speaking of bad attitude," I said, "I understand that you have worked with law enforcement agencies to help them solve crimes."

Mary Ann rattled off several city, state, and federal law enforcement agencies for which she had done work through the years, all without remuneration. She has helped them solve many murder cases and had been given a computer printout of unsolved murders by one police department just in case she happened across the victims' ghosts during her work. She talked about a murder case she had solved in which a nurse had been killed by her husband, her body found in a car after her husband tried to make the crime look to be a car-jacking. Although the police suspected the husband all along, they could not get any evidence on him. The detectives asked Mary Ann for help and took her to the crime scene, showed her photos of the victim, and tried to give her enough information to work with, but nothing worked; Mary Ann needed to talk with the ghost. Some time later the murdered woman's mother received a phone call from her son who was in the military overseas. Her son told her he had had a dream in which he was told that someone with the name "Maria, Mariana, Marian, something like that," could help solve the case. When the mother heard about Mary Ann she contacted her immediately. A few days later the mother, accompanied by the murdered woman's daughter, came to Mary Ann's house. Along with the daughter came the ghost of her mother. The ghost told Mary Ann that her husband had killed her—told her exactly how it had been done, and told her where the police could find the physical evidence they needed to arrest the husband. Mary Ann directed the detectives to an unused storage area in the basement of the victim's apartment, and there they found what they needed to close the case. The husband was arrested and convicted of murdering his wife.

But an even stranger case involved the ghost of a Drug Enforcement Agency officer that Mary Ann had worked with in the past. This time, the ghost showed up in her bedroom.

"You know how kids wake up in the middle of the night and come into your bedroom and stand by your bed staring down at you?" Mary Ann said. "Well, we were asleep and I felt somebody watching me. I look up and there's this guy standing there. I reached over and put my glasses on. He looked at me and said my name and I said, 'What are you doing in my bedroom?' and he said, 'I'm Bill,' and he told me what his last name was and he said I had done some work for him and his partner.

"He said, 'You have to do me a big favor.' I said, 'Like what?' He said, 'I'm going to give you a phone number. Call my partner and tell him where my body is, my wife needs to find my body.' I grabbed the phone and called his partner who said, 'Doggone! Bill listened to me. We had talked about it after you had done work for us. We said if anything ever happened to one of us, we should find you so that we could find each other.' I said, 'That was a wise thing to do.' After that, they found his body."

Mary Ann is rarely publicly credited for her work with police departments because the public would not be accepting of such unusual practices in crime-solving. "I'm always the anonymous tip," she said.

Mary and I were both interested in knowing more about the television show *Ghost Whisperer* and how Mary Ann was involved with it. Her name appears in the credits as a consultant, and she was quick to remind us that the television show is entertainment, stories inspired by her life but not precisely based upon it. She'd been to Los Angeles a few times to work with the writers and actors, and she was satisfied overall with the way in which the show depicted a woman with her special abilities.

"I think people are learning something from the show," Mary Ann said. "I think each week they are seeing something in it. Just admitting that this could possibly exist is a good thing."

"What things do you think people are learning, specifically?" I asked.

"You don't sit on a ghost," she said. "A ghost doesn't walk through you. They move. They don't use windows; they use doors. They used doors when they were alive; they use doors when they're dead. They can't kill you and they can't choke you. I wouldn't be going into people's houses and doing this if they could."

"Can ghosts move things?" Mary asked.

"They can move things, but they can't do it all the time. They have more energy around a full moon. They are electric. They don't use electric, but they conduct it. They don't eat, they don't sleep. They need human energy to keep going."

"That's not how ghosts are usually portrayed on television or in the movies," I said.

Mary Ann laughed. "That's right. They're not bloody and they never carry their heads. They don't do things like that. The body is what's mangled, never the soul."

"I'm sure you've seen some of the other ghost programs on TV," I said. "Ghost Hunters and shows like that on the Discovery and Sci Fi channels. What do you think about those types of paranormal investigations?"

"I feel so sorry for them because I don't have to take anything with me," Mary Ann said. "Either I see the ghosts or I don't and it's really odd because I've been in a room with people who have all that equipment and they'll go stand in a corner someplace and say, 'Oh my gosh, look at this meter going nuts! There's a ghost standing right there!' and I'll be going, 'I don't see it.' But again, maybe they are picking up on something that I can't see, so I never say never because you just don't know. Still, I clean up a lot of these people's messes."

"What do you think of the religious methods some of these people use to get rid of ghosts?"

Mary Ann lowered her voice, perhaps out of respect for the religious beliefs of the other diners who might overhear her words. "I personally would never go into a house throwing holy water around saying, 'In the name of the Lord Jesus, leave here.' It really ticks the ghosts off. I think you're asking for trouble. First, I tell people to call a priest or minister, have the house blessed. It's one thing if a working priest or minister does it, but it's another thing if a layperson does it. The other thing is to get smudge sticks like the Native Americans use. Doing these two things might move the ghosts along. If nothing else, it will make them very lethargic, very laid back, so you're going to see a difference. The house is going to feel better."

"Do you ever just stop and think about your life?" I asked. "How it may have been different if you did not have these gifts?"

Mary Ann laughed. "Oh, sure. Remember I started out as a pet groomer. I guess I think everything happens for a reason. This is just the path that I guess I'm supposed to be on. If you've got a really ornery ghost in your house, your life could be hell, okay? It makes a difference in people's lives to have their house finally cleared up and their life back on track. It makes you feel good."

The three of us talked a little longer as we finished our lunch and I was struck again by Mary Ann's unpretentious and humble personality. By the time we finished our lunch and were putting on our coats in the restaurant lobby, I felt as though I had known Mary Ann for years, rather than minutes. We hugged goodbye and watched Mary Ann drive off in her Cadillac.

Less than 10 minutes later and in full view of the restaurant, I drove our rental car into a losing engagement with a semi on the interstate, completely totaling the car. Amazingly, perhaps protected by spirits, Mary and I walked away showered with broken glass but otherwise unscathed.

"Too bad Mary Ann wasn't a psychic," my wife said. "She could have warned us."

I was interested in knowing more about Mary Ann's adventures in Tinseltown, so two weeks after meeting with her I spoke by phone with John Gray, the creator and executive producer of *Ghost Whisperer*. He spoke to me from his New York office. He told me that someone at CBS who knew the famous psychic medium James Van Praagh (a friend of Mary Ann's) connected him with Mary Ann. They initially met in a Starbucks in Los Angeles.

"I walk into Starbucks, first of all," John said. "I look around and I just don't see anybody who looks like they could be someone who sees dead people. I walked back outside again and I waited and waited, then went back again and then I saw this woman sitting there with this burly guy with a brush-cut and I thought, 'Could that be Mary Ann? I don't know.' I walked over and sure enough, it was her, and I thought this was so funny. She was the least-likely looking ghosthunter you ever met, this down-to-earth, real person. And her husband's the same thing. He's like this salt-of-the-earth kind of guy.

"So we started talking and I just loved how completely casual she was about the whole thing. She wasn't taken with herself; she didn't speak in mystic sort of sentences. She was just very, very real. I asked her whether her ability was something she just sort of turns off and on, does she just see spirits everywhere, does she have to be in a certain mood as it were? She said, 'No, no, I see them pretty much the way I see normal people. They're everywhere.'

"And I said, 'You mean like here?' and she said, 'Oh, sure.'

"I said, 'There's spirits here, in Starbucks.' She said, 'Yeah, there's like three right over there,' and she points and there's a few people sitting by themselves at tables and she goes on to explain who's with them— 'There's an older guy, looks like he's probably the father and over there, there's somebody who could be an ex-boyfriend, I don't know,' and she

Embedded with the Paranormal Paramilitary
Riding with Mediums, Spirit Seekers, and Ghost Hunters
210

proceeds to describe each of the spirits she saw in the Starbucks. In spite of myself, I could feel the hair on the back of my neck kind of go up. I thought, 'Well, that's my first scene, I think,' and I was hooked from that moment on."

I asked him exactly how Mary Ann functions as a consultant. He told me that she has been "a great, great resource," as she reads all the scripts, offering her comments and suggestions, not all of which are accepted.

"I'm sure, in all honesty, at times she probably gets a little frustrated with us because we do try to stretch the story a little bit for the sake of drama. As I always point out, we're not making a documentary about the ghost world. We want it to be logical and we want Mary Ann to feel that it's as realistic as possible, but ultimately, if we come up with a fantastic image or idea and she says that would never happen, but we feel like it's just great for the show, we're probably going to do it. I think Mary Ann is cool with that. I think she gets the joke, that it's fun."

I asked John if anything unusual had happened on the set since he had been working with Mary Ann, and he said that he didn't know of anything, but he did go on to tell me that he and his fiancée had an encounter with ghosts while he was writing the pilot episode of *Ghost Whisperer*, the one whose opening scene is set in a coffee shop. The couple had just purchased an older home outside New York City and, shortly after moving in, began hearing odd sounds. At first, John chalked them up to the typical sounds of an old house, but they began to occur more often and started taking on recognizable and disturbing qualities.

"At night we would hear what sounded so much like footsteps coming up our stairs," John said. "Then we started hearing what sounded like furniture being moved above our heads, up in the attic."

An apartment-dweller for most of his life, John was accustomed to hearing sounds from tenants living above him, but this was different. Who would be living in his attic? John called Mary Ann for advice. She said that she could tell him over the phone whether or not his house was haunted, but she was uncertain when she could actually come out to the New York house to check it out in person.

"Okay," John told her, "don't tell me anything now because if you can't come out here like tomorrow, I don't want to know that I've got ghosts, okay?"

A few days later John flew to Los Angeles to begin filming the pilot, leaving his fiancée back in New York. One night around midnight he received a phone call from her. "It was 3 a.m. her time," John said, "and she was having these really frightening experiences. The car alarms of the cars in the driveway started going off, the doorbell started ringing in the middle of the night and there was no one there. At one point she clipped the wire that led to the doorbell because she couldn't get it to stop ringing and went back upstairs, but it rang again. I could hear all these things going on behind her. She was just freaking out, so I had her come out to L.A. with me."

After the filming was done the couple returned to New York and John flew Mary Ann out to their home to investigate it.

"Right away she found two ghosts in the house," Gray told me. "Mother and son. She said they were not happy, they didn't get along well with each other, and they didn't like me as much as they liked the other owners of the house. It was just amazing. She got a lot of details from them about where they were buried, where they lived, and some really scary things, one of them being that my 12-year-old daughter—who splits her time between my ex-wife's house and my house, both in the same town—had a ghost following her, a really very unhappy little boy. She felt that he was not a good spirit and that it was important that he be detached from my daughter.

"She started telling me that this boy was telling her that he lived in a house which was a home for difficult kids and that he had died. He had fallen out of a window, and mentioned the town that he lived in. None of this made any sense to me but I talked to my ex-wife later that day and told her what Mary Ann had said to us and that she wanted us to protect her house as well.

"When I told her the story," John continued, "my ex-wife got completely still and she said that there was a home for boys right across the road from her house. She later went online and found a news story about a kid who had murdered a boy by pushing him out the window. The kid was now in jail and the boy came from the same town that this supposed ghost told Mary Ann he came from. I mean, it just freaked us out."

John said that Mary Ann had no difficulty in getting the ghosts to cross over and that the house has been quiet since then.

"Are you now a believer in ghosts?" I asked.

"I have always been open to the idea that there is more out there than we know about and I really do believe that love can transcend death. There are people who feel their loved ones around them in certain moments. I really do believe that. To go further than that, I just don't know. I certainly am completely convinced by what Mary Ann says and does. I don't see any other explanation for it.

"I just think we'll never know until we ourselves die, but I do feel personally that there is something else that goes on. I don't think I could ever hope to understand it all while I'm alive, but I do think there's some magic out there."

Chapter 20

Sleeping with Miss Lily

On my first night at the St. Francis Inn in St. Augustine, Florida, I lay awake in bed, listening to the sound of horses' hooves echoing on the cobblestone streets while the voices of the carriage drivers floated up to me: Up there on the third floor is Miss Lily's room. Lily was a black slave who fell in love with the white nephew of the owner of the inn, and since their love could never be, she hung herself in that very room. Her ghost haunts the inn to this day.

I was sleeping, or trying to sleep, in Miss Lily's room.

All I knew about the St. Francis Inn when I made my reservation was that it was haunted. I didn't know by whom or why it was haunted, but I don't like to know all the details about a haunted location before I visit it anyway, preferring to find out for myself, so that was fine with me. I had been in touch with Reverend Dianne Frazier, an empathic psychic (one who can sense and communicate with spirits emotionally and mentally) prior to my visit to Florida, and she had recommend I stay at the St. Francis Inn.

Originally built in 1791 by Señor Gaspar Garcia, the inn stands on the corner of St. George and St. Francis Streets in the heart of St. Augustine's historic district. It is constructed of native coquina limestone, a quarried stone made of compressed shells. A stone and wrought-iron fence separates the inn's courtyard from the street, creating a quiet and lush sanctuary set amidst banana trees, bougainvillea, fragrant jasmine

The St. Francis Inn in St. Augustine, Florida.
Courtesy of John Kachuba.

and other exotic flora. A total of 11 rooms and a two-bedroom cottage comprise the inn, and I was lucky enough to get the ghost's room.

I carried my bags up the creaky old staircase to the third floor, which had formerly been the attic. Miss Lily's room was a small, cozy room located in the corner of the building. Sunlight filtered in through the partially opened shutters that covered each of the floor-to-ceiling windows in the two exterior walls. A fan hung from the white, pressed-tin ceiling. A large, four-poster bed covered with a white chenille bedspread filled one corner. Three bookshelves, stocked with an eclectic collection of titles, were built into the wall alongside the bed. There were two chairs with a small occasional table, and a dresser that supported a television and a cut-glass decanter of sherry. A pedestal sink stood near one of the windows. A door by the sink opened into a closet-sized space that contained the toilet and a claw-foot bathtub with shower attachment.

It was late afternoon when I arrived at the inn. The third floor was quiet and still. I knew by now that Miss Lily was a resident ghost—al-

Miss Lily's room at the St. Francis Inn in St. Augustine, Florida.
Courtesy of John Kachuba.

though I didn't have the ghostly details—and that I was staying in her room, alone, and it occurred to me that if Miss Lily were truly present, it might be wise to let her know my intentions. Even before unpacking, I sat in one of the chairs and spoke to the room. Aloud, I told Miss Lily that I had come to the inn to do some research for a book and that I meant her no harm; I was simply sharing her space for a while. In fact, I said, she might be able to assist me if she was so inclined, because I would be writing about her; perhaps I could hire her as a real ghost-writer. There was no reply from Miss Lily, so I assumed we had reached an understanding of sorts.

Still, that first night I slept fitfully, waking every now and then at unexpected sounds, hearing again in my head the ghost tour carriage drivers' refrain: She hung herself in that very room. I had been up since 3 a.m. in order to catch my flight to Florida, so at some point, sleep finally found me and I was dead to the world.

The next morning, after the rare pleasure (for a Yankee in November) of enjoying breakfast at an outdoor table beneath banana trees, I set off on a walk around St. Augustine, taking in the historic sights, immersing myself in the ambience of America's oldest city. All that was preparation for Dianne Frazier's visit later that day.

That afternoon I was back in my room leafing through some literature about local historic sites when someone knocked on the door. I opened it, and Dianne, followed by her 13-year-old son, Ares, breezed into the room as if we had all been friends for many years.

Reverend Dianne Frazier at Castillo San Marcos in St. Augustine, Florida.
Courtesy of John Kachuba.

Dianne was an energetic and talkative woman with long blond hair and blue eyes. She had a way of looking at you that seemed to penetrate right inside you and come out the other side; it convinced me that she had no trouble at all communicating with spirits.

"I brought something for Miss Lily," Dianne said, showing me two necklaces of cheap costume jewelry, one made of shiny gold beads, the other metallic blue beads. "I always bring her gifts. Let's see which one she prefers." Dianne placed one strand on the table, the other on the dresser. "We won't touch them," she said, "but we'll check them in a few minutes with the meter and see if we get any activity."

Dianne seated herself in one of the chairs while Ares flopped across the bed, EMF meter in hand, running it across the bed and along the wall. "He's still young, but he's learning to develop his abilities as well," Dianne said.

"Catch anything?" I said to Ares.

"No, not yet," he said.

Dianne proceeded to tell me that she and Ares visited St. Augustine often from their home in Jacksonville, and that they had often stayed in Miss Lily's room at the inn. Dianne said that Miss Lily was partial to jewelry and cosmetics and that female guests frequently found their cosmetic bags upset and the contents spilled out.

"She did it to me once," Dianne said, "and I told her to just tell me what she wanted. I would bring it for her next time. I've gotten readings in the bed and I've gotten readings when I've left her presents. She's done things in here like turn off the TV. Some people make fun of her and she'll pack up their bags and leave them by the door."

"Really?" I asked, as I seated myself in the chair opposite Dianne. I dragged the little table between us closer so that I could rest my tape recorder on it, and Dianne gave me a horrified look.

"She doesn't like it when people move things around," she said to me in a low voice. Then speaking to the room she said, "It's okay, Miss Lily. We'll put it right back where it belongs when we're finished."

I felt sufficiently scolded.

"This is her room," Dianne explained. "This is her place where she stayed... I've talked to her about why she was here and she said, 'I've lost him once, I'm not going to lose him again.' She wants to stay here where she has him.

"When people keep the place the same, it's a happy place. Where they run into trouble is when they move things around. There are spirits that are attached to a place and if you go in there and start moving everything around and redoing it, or making renovations, then you're going to start having problems."

I had heard this theory before, especially regarding old buildings that had been undergoing restoration. It seems ghosts just don't like change.

"Let's check the necklaces," Dianne said. She took the EMF meter from Ares and passed it over the two necklaces. I could see the red pointer moving back and forth across the face of the meter, but it wasn't detecting any unusually high electromagnetic frequencies. "Just leave the necklaces out overnight," Dianne said, handing the meter back to Ares, who was still relaxing on the bed, "see if they're moved at all."

We took our seats once more and I asked her how she had become a medium. Dianne said that she had been aware of her abilities all her life but that it was only about 10 years ago when strange things such as lights flashing on and off began happening to her and she started questioning her true purpose in life.

"I don't know if you believe in synchronicity or not," Dianne said, "but synchronicity says that we're guided toward what we're supposed to be doing while we're here. We're supposed to be doing certain things, learning certain things while we're here. While these things were happening to me, all of a sudden there was a story in the newspaper about a paranormal group very close to my house. I started taking ghosthunting classes and went through a bunch of those."

Dianne's curiosity was piqued and she started spending her weekends at the Cassadaga Spiritualist Camp, where she studied various paranormal topics, all designed to increase and strengthen her psychic abilities. She also became an expert in spirit photography, a Reiki master, and an ordained minister through Universal Brotherhood. In addition to working on her own, Dianne is a member of the Florida Paranormal Research Foundation, serving on their spiritualist team.

"The spiritualist team consists of a psychic and support people who take pictures and do some readings to see if the psychic actually did clear the house," Dianne explained. "The psychic, me, goes in with the intention of communicating with the spirits, trying to find out who is there, why they are there, what their issues are, and trying to help them cross over if possible. If not, at least to make conditions livable for both parties—the people who live there and the spirits as well."

"Mom," Ares called from the bed, "she's here."

"Who?" I asked, feeling a shudder run through me.

"Miss Lily," Ares said. He was lying on his left side on the bed and was passing the meter up and down, from head to toe, over the empty space before him. "See, here are her feet," he said, holding the meter near his own feet, "and here's her head, right on the pillow."

Dianne was nonplussed. I didn't know what to say, although my mind was screaming, Holy crap! Holy crap! Holy crap! I've been sleeping with a ghost! It was an odd experience, to say the least. The chairs in which Dianne and I sat were close to the bed so we didn't need to get up to get a better look. There wasn't anything to see, anyway. Yes, it seemed the meter was showing some activity, but nothing felt different to me. Ares was completely nonchalant as he lounged mere inches away from the ghost; obviously this was one 13-year-old who had been around ghosts many times before. Then I guess she was gone. The meter fell back to within a normal range and that was that.

After a few moments of trying to clear my brain, I still wasn't sure what had happened, whether or not the ghost of Miss Lily had truly visited us. I asked Dianne why the ghost would want to make contact with us.

"To me, it makes perfect sense to want to try and communicate," Dianne said. "They don't want to hurt you; they just want to communicate with you, that's all. Just imagine how you'd feel if no one could see you, or hear you, how frustrated, how sad you'd be. That's why, if you can communicate with them, they like to come around. That's why you can attract them. They can tell whether people can see them, hear them, or feel them, so once you start developing your abilities, you might have a bunch come into your home."

A cheery thought.

"I think we all have abilities of some sort," Dianne continued, "but it's in your mental attitude, your approach. If you're a fearful person, you're not going to believe in things you can't control, so therefore, you're not going to allow that. People say to me, 'Eww, you go into cemeteries late at night, that's so scary,' or 'I don't believe in ghosts.' Well, whether you believe in them or not, they're there, and wherever you go they can be there.

"I think it's neat to know that when we love people, even though they've passed on, we can still talk to them and we can still have a relationship with them. They're still part of our lives. It comforts you to know they're still there."

We talked a little longer, and then Dianne and Ares offered to show me around some of St. Augustine's haunted spots. It was almost 11 p.m. before I got back to my room. I stood looking at the bed a long time before finally deciding I would sleep in it. I thought that if Miss Lily had already napped in it earlier, maybe she would let me have it for the night. She must have thought I was too tired, or maybe had a headache, because she did leave me alone all night.

I was checking out the next day and had hoped to talk about the ghost with Bev Lonergen, a manager at the St. Francis Inn who had been working there for 18 years. Unfortunately, Bev was off that day, although I did manage to speak with her by phone once I had returned to Ohio. I asked her if she had ever run into Miss Lily. Bev told me that, not only had she seen Miss Lily, she had seen the ghost of her lover as well.

But before she told me about him, she told me that Miss Lily's story was not as clear as the ghost tour guides made it seem. She said that the love story was true, but that no one really knew if Miss Lily had hung herself, or whether it was her lover who had hung himself, or whether one, or perhaps both of them, had killed themselves by jumping out the window. Bev suspected that the more likely scenario was that the innkeepers at that time simply gave the pregnant Miss Lily some money and sent her away, never to see her lover again. In any case, the ghosts are there.

Bev also told me that the name Lily was determined by a psychic who had come to the inn several years ago and had detected the ghost in the closet—now housing the air conditioner—in what is today called Miss Lily's room.

Great. I had a ghost in the closet and didn't even know it.

Bev has only seen Miss Lily's ghost from the rear. "She won't let me see her face," Bev said. "When I see her, it's very fast. Once on the second floor I saw the back of her dress, and she was small with black hair, very coarse. She had on a pale blue top and black pants and I remember they were very short on her. She was carrying something. I didn't know if was towels for the room or a baby, it was that fast."

Bev's first thought was that she was seeing one of the housekeepers, but when she checked she found she was alone on that floor.

"I've seen her lover as well," Bev said. "During a night shift I was downstairs in the dining room, figuring the books for the next day, and I could see something from the side of my eye and I turned around fast and there he was, standing by the desk area. He had a three-pointer hat and uniform on and he was very small. He had britches on and a coat, and they were red and blue. I remember shiny gold buttons on the coat. He just smiled and then disappeared."

Bev told me that another person had also seen the uniformed ghost. During a major renovation at the inn some years ago, one of the workmen, a man named Harold, asked Bev if she had ever seen a ghost at the inn. Bev said she had and asked him why he wanted to know. Because, replied Harold, he had just seen one, too. Bev let him tell his story first, and Harold said that he had seen a small soldier leaning against a beam on the second floor. Harold's description of the ghost's attire matched that of the ghost Bev had seen.

One of the most common manifestations of the ghosts, Bev said, was their whisperings. The first time Bev heard it was several years ago when she was helping one of the housekeepers split a king-sized bed into its two components. They were working in a room on the second floor when Bev heard someone whispering right behind her.

"Did you hear that?" Bev asked the other woman.

"I sure did," the woman said, running out of the room.

There was no one else on that floor besides the two women.

"I hear the whispering all the time," Bev says. "It's definitely a male voice."

Whispering, huh? On the morning of the day I checked out of the St. Francis Inn I was sitting on the bed packing some things into my suitcase. Suddenly, coming from the corner behind me and sounding very close to my ear, I heard whispering. A deep, masculine tone, although individual words were indistinguishable. A few seconds later, they were gone. I turned around, wondering, What the heck was that? Of course, there was nothing there. Perhaps I had been luckier on my visit to the inn than I had thought. Could it be that not only Miss Lily, but also her lover had visited me?

Chapter 21

Ghosts on Tour

From the many television programs featuring ghosthunters, it would seem that one would require both an immense knowledge of things paranormal and a small fortune to outfit oneself with the latest electronic gear in order to hunt ghosts. Fortunately, that's not the case. Anyone can become a ghosthunter.

One way in which people first get their paranormal feet wet is to take a ghost tour. They can be found all over the United States, in small burgs such as Canal Fulton, Ohio, or venerable old cities such as Savannah and St. Augustine, or major metropolises including Chicago and New York. Usually led by folks who know the local history inside and out, and who are excellent storytellers and ghosthunters, ghost tours come in a wide variety of formats and price ranges. There are walking tours, hiking tours, van and coach bus tours, horse-drawn carriage tours, trolley tours, and even schooner tours. The tours take place in historic city blocks and little town squares, in cemeteries, in abandoned prisons and mental asylums, on battlefields, onboard ships—anywhere and everywhere there was once human activity is a likely location for a ghost tour.

As I've researched my books, I've had the occasion to take part in several ghost tours. I joined ghosthunter and author Troy Taylor on one of his walking tours of Alton, Illinois; rode the bus with Psychic Sonya to haunted locations in downtown Cleveland, Ohio; trekked dark paths through Rogue's Hollow, also in Ohio, with ghosthunter Sherri Brake-Recco; and wandered old Parkersburg, West Virginia streets and

A paranormal hitchhiker on Psychic Sonya's Haunted Cleveland tour.
Courtesy of John Kachuba.

cemeteries with Susan Sheppard. Every time I was amazed by the diversity of people hoping to catch a glimpse of Casper. They ranged from adolescents to senior citizens, from firm believers in ghosts to die-hard skeptics, ghost tour veterans to virgins.

I asked Troy Taylor, the godfather of ghost tours, what makes them popular. Why do people go on ghost tours?

"That's a good question," Troy said. "When we started in 1994, there were only three tours in the entire state of Illinois [Troy's home state], now they're everywhere, all across the country. People are fascinated with ghosts and hauntings, especially when you get into an area with any history at all. When ghost tours are offered people are going to take that ghost tour before they take something else—an architectural tour, for example. That's just the way people are made, that's just the way they're wired, and the interest in ghosts just keeps growing.

"The other thing is that a lot of cities are starting to realize that and have become a lot more open to people doing ghost tours, and for that reason, a lot more of them are springing up. Cities have finally woken up to the idea that it doesn't matter why people are coming to their cities, as long as they are coming and spending money. Tourism is often a cottage industry; it's a great industry, and ghost tours are just part of that."

Troy should know. A review of his website describes his four-city ghost tours in Illinois—Alton, Chicago, Decatur, and Springfield—with two more planned in 2007. He also runs overnight tours to such places as Gettysburg, Baltimore, and Bell Witch sites in Tennessee. When I asked him how many people he has taken on ghost tours, Troy replied, "Thousands and thousands; I couldn't even give you a count."

Allyson Forsythe was the former director of marketing for New Orleans Ghost Tours and has also had experiences with ghost tours in St. Augustine, Florida.

I asked her why so many people signed up for ghost tours, and she replied, "Curiosity. Everyone wants to know if there is something more, and what happens once they leave this Earth. Some go for the thrill and in hopes of being scared. Some go to seek answers to personal experiences with the paranormal."

Do people really experience ghosts on ghost tours? I was on one of Sherri Brake-Recco's tours of Rogue's Hollow in Ohio when several people saw the shadowy figure of a man moving along the forested ridge above the hollow.

While I was inside a haunted theatre in Cleveland traveling with Psychic Sonya, some people saw a figure in the darkened balcony; Sonya casually dismissed it by saying that it was a regular ghost, nothing out of the ordinary!

Sherri Brake-Recco at haunted Rogues' Hollow.
An ember, or perhaps a spirit orb, floats by.
Courtesy of Sherri Brake-Recco.

Troy Taylor tells of the shadow that walked behind him on several consecutive visits to the haunted First Unitarian Church during his walking tour of Alton, Illinois. One night, the shadow was clearly silhouetted against a glass door, but when the tour group went into the other room to see who was casting the shadow, the room was empty. Will Alexander used to host a walking tour of haunted Nantucket and reported seeing lights inside empty houses that had no electricity.

Ursula Bielski, a writer, ghost investigator, and operator of Chicago Hauntings, told me the scariest ghost tour story I have ever heard. Chicago's Hull House, founded by Jane Addams, has a haunted reputation; I wrote about it in my book Ghosthunting Illinois. Ursula had been to the house many times, but had never been in the courtyard behind the building, a courtyard that was rumored to be the site of a portal, a metaphysical gate to the spirit world that allowed spirits to come and go. Ursula led a tour to Hull House, went into the courtyard, and brought a ghost home with her. She awoke at 4 a.m. to find a headless man standing on her bed.

Gray's Armory is one of the stops on Psychic Sonya's Haunted Cleveland tour.
Courtesy of John Kachuba.

"I was absolutely terrified," Ursula said. "I couldn't move, but I could see the clock radio and the man stood there for eight or nine minutes. When I realized it wasn't going anywhere, I started waving my hands in front of me and it stepped back as if to get out of my way. I finally said in this little voice, 'Please go away,' and he put his arms out to the side and then lickety-split he flew backwards and up and dissipated into the ceiling. I slept on the couch for four days. It was very unsettling."

Yes, even for a ghosthunter.

Despite Ursula's encounter, she realizes that ghost tours attract more than just ghosthunters. "I think that a ghost tour is an appealing thing for many more people than just people who are interested in ghosts," she said. "It's an alternative way to look at a place you're visiting. Normally, it's more in-depth, it's more historical, and it's more hands-on.

You usually have an opportunity to go into places and get a look at the architecture and the culture."

In the four years since she and her husband David Cowan started their Chicago tours, approximately 13,000 people have taken them, a number I think that proves Ursula's point that everyone can appreciate a ghost tour.

If you're looking for more information about ghost tours, or if you simply want to find out what's going on in America's paranormal world, the Internet is an incredible resource. One new site, Paranormal Underworld, is making the link between real-life and virtual reality. Juli Velazquez, president and founder of the International Society of Paranormal Investigators, is also Paranormal Underworld's CEO. Juli's team follows paranormal experts as they conduct investigations in haunted locations. Subscribers to the site can watch the investigation unfold before their eyes live, uncut, and unedited. They can also interact with the investigators through the computer in real-time.

You can also find paranormal investigative groups in your area on the Internet and can engage in conversations about all things paranormal. You can buy haunted items, including actual haunted houses, on eBay and other sites. You can register for ghost conferences and ghosthunting lessons and can buy ghost books, ghosthunting equipment, ghost gift items, and spooky music. You can view ghost photos and video clips and can listen to EVPs and paranormal radio programs or podcasts.

A podcast is a multimedia file distributed over the Internet for playback on personal computers or mobile devices such as iPods or MP3 players. The podcast phenomenon is new but is spreading quickly; I searched for "ghosts" and generated 88 results. I had already been a guest on several of the shows on the list, "Ghostly Talk," "The Lou Gentile Show," and "Explore Your Spirit" among them. One aspect of podcasts that makes them so popular among Internet users is that the programs are often archived on their respective websites for a long time, sometimes as long as a year. That means that users never need worry about missing a show; they're still available in the archives.

In a similar vein, I performed a search for "ghost cams," Internet video feeds from cameras placed in haunted locations. I found sites that allowed me to spy for ghosts inside the *Queen Mary*, the Willard Library in Evansville, Indiana, the Paris catacombs, and assorted asylums, prisons, and castles. No doubt spurred by popular television ghosthunting programs, ghost cams are popping up everywhere on the Internet. I even thought about mounting a camera on the dashboard of my Ghosthuntermobile, so that my readers could travel along with me on my ghosthunting treks, but I couldn't figure out the technical logistics.

I am not a novice when it comes to working on a computer or surfing the Internet, but as I began to research my ghost books a few years ago, I realized I was completely unaware of the sheer amount of paranormal material that is available online. In no time at all, I was talking with ghost groups all across the country—all across the world, in fact—and posting messages and comments on various message boards.

There are so many paranormal websites popping up on a daily basis that some Web designers have begun to specialize in designing sites for the paranormal audience. Shelley Sullivan is one such entrepreneur. Shelley lives in Honolulu, Hawaii, and is the owner of Spooktacular Designs. Shelley's interest in ghosts began when she lived in a haunted house in Guam. Later, she lived in Tennessee and founded a ghosthunting group.

"I have experience in the paranormal investigative area," Shelley said. "I know what needs to be done, what needs to be presented; I know how reports need to be presented. This is especially helpful for ghost groups that are new, just starting out. I like other groups' sites to look professional instead of having everything all over the place, not knowing where to go, the navigation being really sucky, if you'll pardon that expression. I like for them to be able to present the paranormal research field in a professional manner."

After looking at so many websites, I decided that I needed to build one for my ghost books. To avoid some of the mess typical of many websites, I asked Amy Yosmali of AY Design to create mine. My website was the first paranormal site Amy had ever designed, although she had designed sites for other clients; you can take a look at it for yourself and let me know what you think. In fact, I'm currently looking for stories about international ghosthunting, so feel free to post one on the site.

A sucker for popular culture, I could not resist setting up another website where I could converse with fellow ghosthunters and readers of ghost books, which has been an amazing experience. Within one month's time, over five hundred people had become my "friends," and I had received invitations to speak on radio programs and at conferences, to cross promote my books with music CDs, and to work on some documentary television programs. Plus, I've met a lot of fascinating people.

The Internet has revolutionized so many areas of modern life that it is no wonder it has had an enormous impact on the paranormal community. Perhaps in time we won't need to go on ghost tours or ghost hunts because we will be able to contact ghosts directly through the computer. That will bring a whole new meaning to the term the ghost inside the machine.

CHAPTER 22

GHOSTS IN THE CLOSET

W e've all got them. Even if we think that we have absolutely no ghost stories related to our own families, the truth is that we do. Ask enough people, and I would be willing to bet my official ghosthunter hat that you will find a story about your Great Aunt Millie that will turn your hair white.

I discovered this firsthand after I published Ghosthunting Ohio in 2004. While I was driving all over the state of Ohio interviewing countless numbers of people about their ghostly experiences, it never occurred to me to ask anyone in my family about ghosts. After all, the paranormal was not a usual topic of conversation when we were together, nor were any family members, as far as I could tell, particularly interested in the subject.

That's why I was surprised when both my daughters, Kristen and Sarah, told me they had each been involved in ghostly encounters when they were students at the University of Connecticut. They had never said anything to me at the time the events had happened, but waited several years after they had graduated to tell me, apparently stimulated by the publication of my book.

Kristen rather casually mentioned one day that she had been visited by something macabre in her dorm that had terrified her. She said that she had been asleep in the upper bunk in her room, her roommate sleeping below, when she suddenly awoke. Something was lurking at the foot of her bunk.

"It was a black triangular shape that looked something like a head and shoulders beneath a robe," Kristen said. "I couldn't move. I just lay there, staring at it, and then it started moving up over my legs, coming closer. It seemed like I could see eyes and a mouth in the blackness. I was so scared I couldn't speak."

Kristen said that she was finally able to slowly move her hand down from the bunk in an attempt to wake her roommate, and that when she did, the specter vanished. Her roommate did not wake up and the entity never returned.

"What do you think it was?" I asked her.

"I don't know. My immediate thought was that it was Death," Kristen said.

You don't know my daughter, of course, but for her to make such a statement was pretty heady stuff. Kristen is not particularly philosophical or theological. Her naming the thing Death comes more from a visceral, intuitive response than it does from any intellectual formulation.

"Why Death?"

"I don't know, Dad. I was really sick at that time, if you remember, and wound up in the hospital, so maybe my mind was thinking that."

"Could be," I said.

She nodded. "I remember I had a really high fever so maybe that's what caused it. Maybe it was a hallucination."

Maybe it was. Then again, maybe it wasn't. I know that if Kristen were simply making up a story, she wouldn't make up one with ghosts in it. Ghost stories "creep me out" she would say—so much so that she won't even read her own father's books about them.

Then Kristen dropped the other shoe. "Sarah said she saw a ghost too."

This was too much, both of my daughters with personal ghost stories.

When I asked Sarah why she hadn't told me about her ghost story before, she shrugged and said that she just hadn't thought about it. Sarah's story also took place in her dorm room. She too was sleeping in the upper bunk—maybe seeing ghosts in college is an upper-bunk thing. Less oxygen up there, I don't know.

"I heard a loud sigh and turned over to see who it was," Sarah said. "The moon was coming in through the window and I saw a man standing in the middle of the room."

Seeing a strange man standing in your dorm room would be a frightening sight for any coed, but Sarah felt no fear at all. In fact, she felt a sense of peace and well-being.

"I recognized him as Grandpa," Sarah said, "so I just rolled over and went back to sleep."

Her Grandpa Joe had died when Sarah was very young, and I doubt that she had any actual recollections of him. She had seen photos of him, of course, but probably not that many.

"How did you know it was Grandpa Joe?" I asked. "Did it look like him?"

"Not really, Dad," Sarah said. "It was just a man, but there was something about him, I can't explain it, something told me it was him and that I had nothing to worry about."

"Why do you think he was there?"

"I think maybe he just wanted to visit," Sarah said.

There's more.

In the summer of 2005, my wife Mary and I were sitting with my brother, Mike, and his wife, Mary Ellen, on the front porch of their house in Stratford, Connecticut. It was a beautiful July evening. We had just finished dinner and were talking while the cicadas and crickets buzzed and chirped in the night air. The conversation turned to my ghost books and I mentioned how surprised I was to find that, whenever I was in a group of people talking about ghosts, someone would always have a personal story to relate. I had never thought that so many people had bumped into ghosts at some point in their lives.

It was then that Mary Ellen said the house in which she had been raised in Fairfield had been haunted. Before she told us her story, she reminded us that she was of Irish ancestry and that the Irish see ghosts everywhere.

Mary Ellen said that the basement in the old house was used for some storage but that hardly anyone went down into it, except for her brother, who had a model train layout down there. Sometimes he would find little cars and other toys in the basement that did not belong to him. Her brother was particular with his trains, and often when he went down to the basement to play with them he would notice that they were not as he had left them the day before, but had been moved around. Neither his sisters nor his parents said they had been in the basement.

Mary Ellen also said that sometimes her mother would go into the basement and find cartons stacked up against the furnace.

"She was concerned about the fire hazard," Mary Ellen said, "so she moved the boxes away and then told my brother not to put them there. Of course, he said he didn't put them there, nor did my father or my sisters say they had moved the boxes. That happened more than once. She would move the boxes, then, a few days later, see that they were piled there again. She would move them away again."

One day, her mother got so angry that she stood in the basement and called out, "All right, George, that's it! No more!" The boxes stopped moving.

"Why George?" I asked.

"She didn't know why," Mary Ellen said. "The name just came to her."

Some time later, a woman knocked on the door and told Mary Ellen's mother that she had once lived in the house and asked her if she could look around. Mary Ellen's mother let the woman in and walked with her through the house. The woman said that her brother, who was deceased, had also enjoyed playing with trains. Her brother's name, of course, was George.

Strange tales all, I think, but what makes them so interesting is that my family is probably not much different from yours. We don't attend séances, we don't hunt ghosts—okay, so I do, but I'm the exception—we don't think of Halloween as anything more than a masquerade party and an opportunity to stockpile Snickers, and we don't harbor any unnatural fears of cemeteries. Yet, we have our stories. It could be that if you ask around you may discover that your family also has skeletons—make that ghosts—in your closet.

In an age in which families are often scattered over many miles and communication between family members may be infrequent or superficial, exploring ghost stories could foster closer family ties. It seems that everyone loves to hear a good ghost story, and how much more interesting would they be if they actually occurred in your own family? To people you know and love?

Any discussion about ghost stories, especially with family members, can progress far beyond the mere "boo factor" and become much more meaningful. They can open doors to discussions about history, philosophy, and theology. Asking the single question, "Do you believe in ghosts?" sets the stage for other questions that explore the nature of spirituality, the existence of an afterlife, even the nature of God. Without getting too serious here, the point I want to make is that talking about ghost stories with your family will undoubtedly provide you with insights about family members that you never had before. Ghost stories are also a fun way to bridge the intergenerational gap among families in the same manner as obtaining oral histories.

A question that my wife, Mary, and I often discuss is this: If you could come back as a ghost, what sign would you leave for your loved ones so they would know it was indeed you? We have not yet answered that question, and I'm not so sure Mary is necessarily interested in doing so. Perhaps one life with me is enough. In some parts of the Caribbean, widows wear red underwear in the belief that it will keep their dead husbands from returning to them as ghosts. The last time we strolled past a Victoria's Secret store window Mary spent a long time gazing at fancy new underwear.

Red underwear.

Glossary

apparition A ghostlike image of a person.

asylum An institution offering support to the mentally ill.

auditory Of or relating to one's hearing.

clairvoyance The ability to perceive things beyond normal sensory contact.

committed To send someone to be confined in a psychiatric hospital.

corroborate To confirm or give support to.

delusion An impression that is believed despite being contradicted by what is generally accepted as reality.

demonic Characteristic of demons or evil spirits.

electromagnetism The interaction of electric currents or fields and magnetic fields.

ESP Extrasensory perception is perception occurring outside of normal sensory processes.

hallucination A perception of something not present.

hypnosis The state of consciousness in which a person apparently loses the power of voluntary action.

implication A conclusion that can be drawn from something.

infestation Invaded or overrun by organisms or beings.

lunatic Generally, a mentally ill person.

notorious Famous for some bad quality.

occult Supernatural, mystical, or magical beliefs, practices, or phenomena.

olfactory Relating to the sense of smell.

pagan A person who has religious beliefs other than those of the main world religions.

paranormal Phenomena that are beyond the scope of normal scientific understanding.

poltergeist A ghost responsible for physical disturbances.

precognition Foreknowledge of a paranormal event.

preternatural Beyond what is normal or natural.

séance A meeting at which people attempt to make contact with the dead through a medium.

telepathy Communication of thoughts or ideas by means other than the known senses.

FOR MORE INFORMATION

American Society for Psychical Research, Inc. (ASPR)
5 West 73rd Street
New York, NY 10023
(212) 799-5050
Website: http://www.aspr.com

This organization's mission is to explore extraordinary or unexplained phenomena that have been called psychic or paranormal, and their implications for our understanding of consciousness, the universe, and the nature of existence. It addresses questions with scientific research and offers educational activities including lectures and conferences.

Ghost Hunters
Syfy Channel
NBCUniversal Cable Entertainment Group
30 Rockefeller Plaza
New York, NY 10112
(212) 664-4444
Website: http://www.syfy.com/ghosthunters

In each episode of the Ghost Hunters television program, Jason Hawes and his team of paranormal investigators, TAPS (The Atlantic Paranormal Society) investigate paranormal activity across the country.

Parapsychological Association, Inc. (PA)

P.O. Box 24173

Columbus, OH 43224

(202) 318-2364

Website: http://www.parapsych.org

The Parapsychological Association is the international professional organization of scientists and scholars engaged in the study of "psi" (or "psychic") experiences, such as telepathy, clairvoyance, and psychic healing. The PA endorses no ideologies or beliefs other than the value of rigorous scientific and scholarly inquiry.

Rhine Research Center

2741 Campus Walk Avenue

Building 500

Durham, NC 27705

(919) 309-4600

Website: http://rhinecenter.org

The Rhine Research Center's mission is to advance the science of parapsychology, to provide education and resources for the public, and to foster a community for individuals with personal and professional interest in paranormal phenomena and the nature of human consciousness.

WEBSITES

Because of the changing nature of Internet links, Rosen Publishing has developed an online list of websites related to the subject of this book. This site is updated regularly. Please use this link to access the list: http://www.rosenlinks.com/HH/embed

FOR FURTHER READING

Bader, Christopher David., Frederick Carson Mencken, and Joe Baker. *Paranormal America: Ghost Encounters, UFO Sightings, Bigfoot Hunts, and Other Curiosities in Religion and Culture.* New York, NY: New York University Press, 2010.

Belanger, Jeff. *Ghosts of War: Restless Spirits of Soldiers, Spies, and Saboteurs* (Haunted: Ghosts and the Paranormal). New York, NY: Rosen Publishing, 2009.

Buckland, Raymond. *The Weiser Field Guide to Ghosts: Apparitions, Spirits, Spectral Lights, and Other Hauntings of History and Legend.* San Francisco, CA: Weiser Books, 2009.

Booth, B. J. *UFOs Caught on Film: Amazing Evidence of Alien Visitors to Earth.* Newton Abbot, UK: David & Charles, 2012.

Clarke, David. *How UFOs Conquered the World: The History of a Modern Myth.* New York, NY: Aurum, 2015.

Lace, William. *Ghost Hunters* (Library of Ghosts & Hauntings). San Diego, CA: ReferencePoint Press, 2010.

Grant, John. *Spooky Science: Debunking the Pseudoscience of the Afterlife*. New York, NY: Sterling, 2015.

Gudgeon, Christopher. *Ghost Trackers: The Unreal World of Ghosts, Ghost-Hunting, and the Paranormal*. Toronto, ON, Canada: Tundra, 2010.

Matthews, Rupert. *The Little Book of the Paranormal*. Stroud, Glouchestershire, England: History Press, 2010.

Selzer, Adam. *Your Neighborhood Gives Me the Creeps: True Tales of an Accidental Ghost Hunter*. Woodbury, MN: Llewellyn Publications, 2009.

Warren, Ed, Lorraine Warren, and Robert David Chase. *Ghost Hunters: True Stories from the World's Most Famous Demonologists*. New York, NY: St. Martin's, 2014.

INDEX

Embedded with the Paranormal Paramilitary
Riding with Mediums, Spirit Seekers, and Ghost Hunters
246

Embedded with the Paranormal Paramilitary
Riding with Mediums, Spirit Seekers, and Ghost Hunters
250

ABOUT THE AUTHOR

John Kachuba is the author of Ghosthunting Illinois and Ghosthunting Ohio. He lives in Athens, Ohio, reputed to be one of the most haunted towns in the country. He is currently working on a book about international ghosts and ghosthunters, and welcomes hearing any ghost stories from other countries.